Option Strategy Risk / Return Ratios

A Revolutionary New Approach to Optimizing, Adjusting, and Trading Any Option Income Strategy

BRIAN JOHNSON

DEDICATION

I am what I am and who I am today because of the most important person in my life – my wife Linda. Thank you for your unwavering love and support (and editing).

DISCLAIMER

Information in this e-book and in the accompanying spreadsheets is provided solely for informational and general educational purposes and should not be construed as an offer to sell or the solicitation of an offer to buy securities *or to provide investment advice*. Option trading has large potential rewards, but also large potential risk. You must be aware of the risks and be willing to accept them in order to invest in the options markets. Do not trade with money you cannot afford to lose.

CONTENTS

Introduction   1

1   Option Income Strategies   3

2   The Greeks   21

3   Option Strategy Heuristics   42

4   Delta/Theta Risk/Return Ratio (DTRRR)   50

5   Vega/Theta Risk/Return Ratio (VTRRR)   70

6   Rho/Theta Risk/Return Ratio (RTRRR)   89

7   Iron Condors   105

8   Calendar Spreads   119

9   Iron Butterflies   131

10 Double Diagonals   142

11 Hybrid Combinations   153

12 Strategy Summary   171

13 Practical Considerations   181

    About the Author   196

    Resources   197

INTRODUCTION

Written by Brian Johnson, a professional investment manager with many years of trading and teaching experience, *Option Strategy Risk/Return Ratios* introduces a revolutionary new framework for evaluating, comparing, adjusting, and optimizing option income strategies. Drawing on his extensive background in option-pricing and on decades of experience in investment management and trading, Brian Johnson developed these tools specifically to manage option income strategies.

Unlike crude rules-of-thumb, these revolutionary new tools can be applied to any option income strategy, on any underlying security, in any market environment. Risk and return are timeless concepts in finance and trading, but this is the first time both concepts have been integrated successfully into a consistent approach for managing option income strategies.

Option Strategy Risk/Return Ratios is written in a clear, easy-to-understand fashion and explains how to apply risk/return ratios to condors, butterflies, calendars, double diagonals, and even hybrid income strategies.

Created especially for investors who have some familiarity with options, this practical guide begins with an examination of option income strategies and is followed by a review of the option Greeks, the building blocks of option risk management. Next, a critique of common adjustment triggers lays the foundation for a detailed explanation of these exciting new tools: option strategy risk/return ratios.

Each option income strategy is explained, evaluated, and ranked using these new tools with complete descriptions and graphical examples. The book includes over sixty separate graphs and tables to illustrate how risk/return ratios behave using specific strategy examples in actual market conditions.

The risk/return ratios are then used to introduce a new hybrid strategy that combines the best characteristics of the other income strategies. Finally, the last chapter examines practical considerations and prospective applications of these innovative new tools.

Not only are the formulas provided for every calculation, but each risk/return ratio is explained intuitively and depicted graphically. For traders who are not mathematically inclined, *Option Strategy Risk/Return Ratios* also includes the address for a link to an Excel spreadsheet with macros designed to calculate all of the risk/return ratios introduced in the book.

1 OPTION INCOME STRATEGIES

Market-neutral option income strategies are incredibly popular for one simple reason: they make money. What are market-neutral strategies? Market-neutral means that these strategies are neither bullish nor bearish. Market-neutral or non-directional strategies perform equally well, regardless whether the underlying security experiences a comparable increase or decrease in price.

This is very different from directional strategies that only earn positive returns when the market moves in the forecasted direction. Most traders focus almost exclusively on directional strategies. They may vary the holding periods, investment candidates, or technical triggers, but they allocate the majority of their capital to strategies that only earn a profit if the market moves in the desired direction.

As a result, market-neutral strategies offer significant strategy diversification benefits. When the market is trending, directional strategies tend to perform well, but option-income strategies do not. Conversely, during periods of price consolidation, directional strategies often underperform, but option-income strategies do very well. Consequently, allocating capital to both market-neutral and directional strategies can increase your returns and reduce your risk.

This probably seems strange to directional traders. If the market does not move, option income strategies make money. That's right, nothing happens, but you still make money. Unfortunately, option income strategies are complex. There are many exotic sounding option income strategies to choose from: iron butterflies, iron condors, double diagonals, calendar spreads, and many others. Each of these strategies can be constructed from options with a wide range of strike prices and expiration dates, resulting in an overwhelming number of choices for the option trader.

I primarily use equity index options for my option income strategies. Equity index options are extremely liquid and the prices of equity indices are typically much higher than the prices of their corresponding exchange traded funds (ETFs). For example, the price of the S&P 500 index (SPX) is approximately ten times the price of its corresponding ETF (SPY).

As a result, one option contract on SPX is equivalent to approximately ten option contracts on SPY, but the commissions per contract are comparable. Therefore, the commissions from trading options on SPY are nearly ten times the cost of commissions from trading options on SPX. Using large, liquid, equity indices for option income strategies reduces transaction costs, which is critical to the success of these multi-leg positions.

Equity index options also offer tax advantages and simplified IRS reporting requirements. In addition, equity indices are not as exposed to earnings spikes or specific company event risk, both of which could lead to large, discrete price changes that would be treacherous for most option income strategies.

Even if you focused exclusively on equity index options, there would still be a number of unanswered questions. Which option income strategy would be the best? Which strike prices and expiration dates should you use to construct the strategy? Should you adjust the strategy? If so, when? How would the risks of these strategies be affected by the market environment? How would a condor on an equity index compare to a condor on IBM?

Until now, there has never been a consistent, objective framework for answering these types of questions. This book will provide the tools you need to objectively evaluate any option income strategy, on any underlying security, in any market environment. However, before I introduce these new tools, we need to examine how and why option strategies make money. The secret is in the asymmetrical payoff function.

Asymmetrical Payoff Functions

Call and put options have asymmetrical payoff functions. This sounds complicated, but is actually relatively straightforward. A call option gives the owner or buyer the right, but not the obligation, to purchase the underlying asset at the strike price on or before the expiration date. For now, let's keep things simple and ignore the fact that many options can be exercised prior to expiration. This will allow us to focus our attention on what happens at option expiration.

The following example (depicted in Figure 1.1) should help illustrate the concept of asymmetry. If we purchased a one-year call option on IBM with a strike price of $100, we would only choose to exercise the call option if the price of IBM were above the $100 strike price (in the money) on the expiration date.

If the price of IBM were $110 on the expiration date, the payoff would be $10. The payoff is also called the intrinsic value and represents the value of exercising the in-the-money options at expiration. In this case, we could purchase IBM for the $100 strike price and immediately sell it at the market price of $110 for a payoff of $10. If the market price of IBM were $120 on the expiration date, the payoff would be $20. For every dollar the price of IBM rose above the strike price of $100, the payoff of the call option would increase by $1. As a result, the slope of the payoff function above the strike price is plus 1.0 (one dollar increase in payoff for every one dollar increase in the price of IBM).

If the price of IBM were below the $100 strike price (out of the money) on the expiration date, we would choose not to exercise the option and it would expire worthless. In that scenario, the payoff would be zero – although we would incur a loss on the trade.

It is important not to confuse payoffs and profits. Payoff functions (not profit and loss functions) should be used to determine the value of options. It would not matter how much the price of IBM dropped below $100; the call option would expire worthless and the payoff would still be zero. All options that are out of the money on the expiration date expire worthless and therefore have an intrinsic value and payoff of zero. As a result, the slope of the payoff function below the strike price is zero (zero change in the payoff function for a one dollar increase in the price of the underlying security).

Note the discrete change in the slope of the payoff function that occurs at the strike price. The slope of the payoff function is zero when the price of the underlying stock (IBM) is below the strike price ($100) and the slope of the payoff function line is plus 1.0 when the price of the stock is above the strike price. This payoff function is asymmetric and this asymmetry creates value for the call option. To understand how income strategies make money, we need to examine how this asymmetry creates value and how and why that value changes over time.

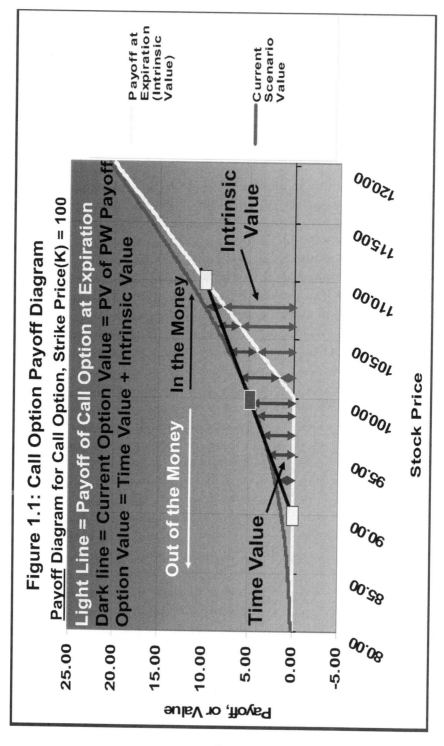

Figure 1.1: Call Option Payoff Diagram

Asymmetry, Option Values & Time Decay

The value of an option represents the present value of its probability-weighted future payoffs. What does that mean? Let's use the IBM call option payoff function from Figure 1.1 again to work through a simple example. First, let's assume that the stock price of IBM today is $100 and that one year from today, there were only two possible states of the world: the price of IBM would either increase by 10% (+ $10) or the price of IBM would decrease by 10% (- $10). In other words, one year from today there would be a 50% probability of IBM closing at $90 and a 50% probability of IBM closing at $110.

The payoffs in those two hypothetical scenarios would be $0 and $10, respectively (see outside boxes in Figure 1.1). Given that the two possible payoffs of $0 and $10 both had a 50% probability of occurring, the average payoff one year from today would be $5 [(50% x $0) + (50% x $10)]. To determine the value of the call option today, we would technically need to discount the probability-weighted payoff of $5 back to the present using a proxy for the risk-free interest rate.

However, as I write this in early 2014, short-term interest rates are approximately zero and have been near zero for several years. Even more important, discounting the expected future payoff would complicate our example unnecessarily and shift our focus away from our primary objective: understanding the effects of asymmetric payoff functions on option values.

To summarize the valuation example, IBM is currently trading at $100. If there were a 50% probability of IBM increasing or decreasing by 10% in one year, the value of a one-year call option with a strike price of $100 would be $5 (ignoring discounting).

Now we are finally ready to understand what happens to option values as time passes, which is the basis for all market-neutral option income strategies. Continuing with our IBM example, let's now assume that six months had passed and the price of IBM had remained unchanged at $100. The original one-year call option would now only have six months remaining until expiration. Assuming the market volatility environment had not changed, would the expected price change of IBM over the next six months be greater or less than our original 12-month assumed price change of plus or minus 10%?

It would be logical to assume that if IBM were expected to

increase or decrease by 10% over 12 months, IBM would be expected to increase or decrease by a lesser amount over six months, perhaps by only 5%. The assumption is logical, but the math would be a little different. I will address the math shortly, but for now, let's assume that IBM was expected to increase or decrease by 5% over the remaining six months.

The call option payoffs in those two new six-month scenarios would be $0 and $5, respectively. Using the same probability assumptions, the average payoff six months from today would be $2.50 [(50% x $0) + (50% x $5)]. If we ignore discounting again in our simplistic example, the value of the IBM call option would have declined from $5 to $2.50.

Since the market price of IBM was exactly equal to the strike price ($100), the intrinsic value would have been zero in both examples. However, the time premium or time value of the original one-year option would have declined by $2.50 over the six-month holding period.

The expected dispersion of prices decreases as time passes, which reduces the value of the asymmetrical payoff function, which means that option values decline over time. This is called time decay and it is measured by Theta, which will be discussed again in the next chapter.

This is how option income strategies make money. They make time decay work to their advantage by selling options (time value or time premium) and managing those positions as the time premium shrinks.

As I mentioned earlier, the time decay function is actually not linear, unlike our simplistic assumption in the preceding example. The expected dispersion of prices in most option models is not limited to two possible outcomes and it is not assumed to be a linear function of time. Instead, price dispersion and time premium are assumed to be increasing functions of the *square root of time*, not of time itself. In other words, the expected dispersion of prices over four months is NOT four times the expected dispersion of prices over one month. In practice, the expected dispersion of prices over four months is assumed to be twice (square root of 4) the expected dispersion of prices over one month.

Figure 1.2 is a graph of the value of an at-the-money (ATM) call option (dotted line) and an ATM put option (dashed line) as a function of time. Time-to-expiration is depicted on the x-axis (horizontal) and the theoretical values of the call and put option relate to the left-hand y-axis (vertical).

Finally, the solid line (middle) represents the square root of the number of days until expiration and these values correspond to the right-hand y-axis (vertical). As you can see from the graph, the values of call and put options are clearly both a function of the square root of time remaining until expiration.

Since the call and put options in Figure 1.2 are at-the-money options, the intrinsic value is zero by definition. That means that the data depicted in the chart represents time value exclusively. Time value decays as a function of the square root of time, so selling time premium is the foundation of option income strategies. But which options should you sell?

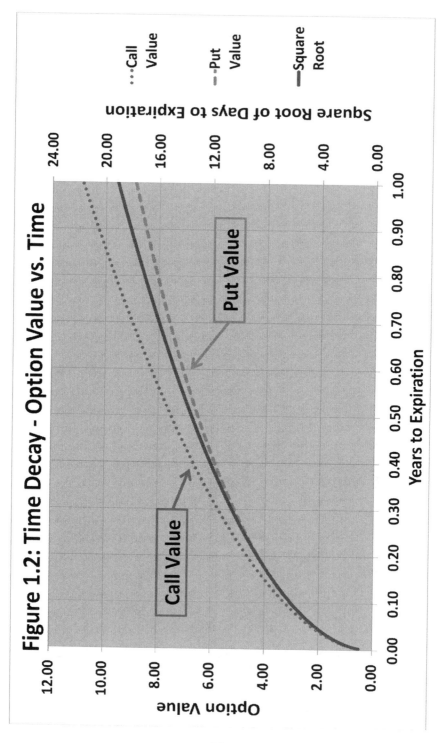

Figure 1.2: Time Decay - Option Value vs. Time

ATM options have the greatest time premium, so it would be logical to sell ATM or near-the-money options and buy out-of-the-money (OTM) options. If selling options allows you to profit from the decay of time value, why buy options at all? Because selling uncovered or naked options would expose you to unacceptable levels of risk and would also require excessive amounts of capital, which would reduce your prospective strategy returns.

As a result, option income strategies typically buy options further out of the money to "cover" their short option positions, which limits their prospective losses and reduces the margin requirement. This reduces the amount of capital required to implement the strategy, reduces risk, and also increases returns. Condors and butterflies (presented in Chapter 7 and Chapter 9) both buy OTM options to cover their short option positions.

However, there is another important insight that can be gleaned from the graph in Figure 1.2: time premium decays more rapidly as options approach expiration. As a result, it would be possible to benefit from time decay by selling an option with less time remaining and buying an option of the same type with more time remaining. This is called a calendar or time spread and it is another tool used in option income strategies.

Proven Option Income Advantage

The fact that options decay over time does not guarantee success or profitability for option income strategies. Selling options, even covered options, involves taking risk. In order to earn excess returns from selling options over time, options must be systematically and consistently overpriced. Many traders overlook this very important point. Are there any reasons that options would be systematically overpriced and are there any empirical data to support that theory? Absolutely.

The most compelling explanation as to why equity index options are chronically overvalued is that traders and investment managers use options to hedge their exposure to the market. There are only two types of traders: hedgers and speculators. Hedging transactions reduce risk and speculative transactions increase risk. In exchange for reducing risk, hedgers are willing to pay a premium when purchasing options. In exchange for taking on a portion of the hedger's risk, speculators (option sellers) demand a premium, just as insurance companies price their policies to earn a profit.

However, not every underlying security is used for hedging purposes, which means options are not systematically overvalued on all underlying securities. Option income strategies should only be employed using options that are chronically overvalued; this guarantees a proven statistical advantage.

How can you determine which underlying securities have options that have historically been overvalued? The easiest way is to compare implied volatility to statistical (also called historical) volatility. When implied volatility is consistently higher than statistical volatility, options for the underlying security are systematically overvalued, which creates a trading advantage for option sellers.

Statistical volatility is expressed as the annualized standard deviation of the percentage price change and is calculated from the actual price changes of the underlying security. Implied volatility is also expressed as the annualized standard deviation of the percentage price change, but it is not calculated from the actual price changes of the underlying security. Instead, it represents the expected level of volatility (price dispersion) that is priced into a specific option. In other words, implied volatility is the level of volatility that is implied by the price of the option; implied volatility is synonymous with option price.

As we saw in the IBM example, higher levels of expected volatility result in higher option prices. Conversely, lower levels of expected volatility mean lower prices. This applies to both calls and puts. Higher implied volatility always equates to higher option prices and vice versa.

When the expected level of volatility priced into an option (implied volatility) is consistently higher than the actual volatility realized over the life of that option, the option would be systematically overvalued. The dashed line in Figure 1.3 represents the statistical volatility (SV) for the S&P 500 index from 2010 through late 2013. The solid line represents the 30-day implied volatility (IV) for options on the S&P 500 index. As you can see from the chart, IV and SV tended to move together, but IV was consistently higher than SV.

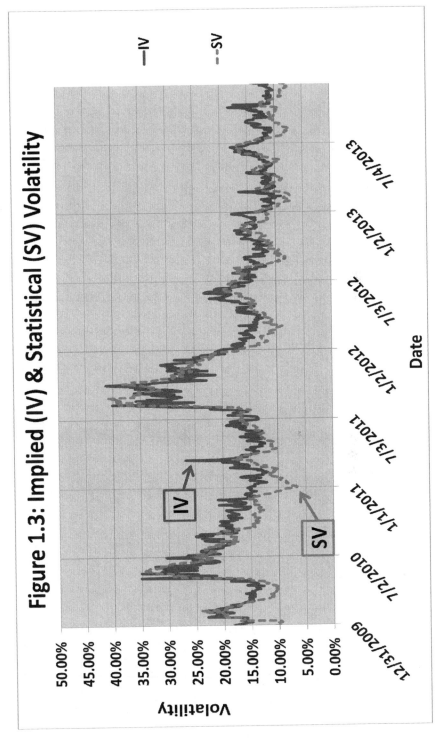

Figure 1.3: Implied (IV) & Statistical (SV) Volatility

The chart in Figure 1.3 clearly demonstrates the historical relationship between IV and SV for S&P 500 index options, but it does not tell us the actual numerical difference between IV and SV. The average IV and SV values for the data in the Figure 1.3 chart are provided by the table in Figure 1.4.

The IV and SV averages were calculated for seven periods ranging from three weeks to six years. In every case, average implied volatility exceeded average statistical volatility for S&P 500 index options. The average difference between implied volatility and historical volatility across all periods was 2.05%.

Figure 1.4: S&P 500 Implied Volatility (IV) vs. Statistical Volatility (SV)							
Historical Period	3 Weeks	6 Weeks	10 Weeks	1.5 Years	3 Years	4.5 Years	6 Years
Implied Volatility (IV)	11.80%	11.50%	12.10%	13.20%	16.30%	17.70%	21.30%
Statistical Volatility (SV)	8.50%	8.80%	9.80%	11.70%	14.70%	15.80%	20.20%
Difference (IV - SV)	3.30%	2.70%	2.30%	1.50%	1.60%	1.90%	1.10%

At first glance, a difference of 2.05% might not seem significant. However, a 2.05% difference between IV and SV does not mean that options were only overvalued by 2.05%. Overestimating volatility by 2.05% would result in 30-day ATM call and put options that were overpriced by approximately 15%.

The objective of option income strategies is to harvest some of that 15% overvaluation. And the opportunity to capture that excess return is available every month. The recent introduction of weekly options opens up even more income strategy opportunities. I hope you are beginning to see the amazing return potential of employing option income strategies on underlying securities with systematically overvalued options.

The IV and SV data from Figures 1.3 and 1.4 were provided by OptionVue. For more information about OptionVue, please see the Resources section at the end of this book.

Additional Evidence of a Trading Edge

The six-year relationship between IV and SV on S&P 500 index options is noteworthy, but in my proprietary research on option income strategies, I developed a tool that provided comprehensive evidence of a statistical advantage to selling options on equity indices.

I began with the following question: what is the probability advantage of selling out-of-the-money (OTM) equity index options as a function of 1) the length of the holding period and 2) the degree each option is out of the money.

I could have calculated the realized probabilities of each option expiring worthless (out of the money) and compared that to the tail probabilities from a normal distribution function. The simplicity of this approach was appealing, but the implications were simply not practical. This approach implicitly assumed that I would leave short option positions open, even after they moved in the money, hoping that prices would reverse and they would eventually expire worthless. The risk of this trading strategy would be unacceptable.

As a result, I instead calculated the realized probabilities of the price of the underlying security "touching" the strike price of the OTM option sold any time during the holding period. I then compared the realized touch probabilities to the theoretical probabilities of touching the short strike to determine the historical probability advantage or disadvantage. The mechanical details of calculating the theoretical touch probabilities are beyond the scope of this book, but the calculations used 5000-path Monte Carlo simulations from an arbitrage-free binomial lattice.

The following probabilities were calculated on the S&P 500 (SPX), Russell 2000 (RUT), and NASDAQ 100 (NDX) indices from 2000 through late 2013, using rolling holding periods ranging from one day to 60 days. Rolling holding periods means that a new holding period began every day, which means the holding periods overlapped. This provided more observations (over 9000), although the overlapping observations were not independent.

I chose the year 2000 as the starting point to ensure that two bull and two bear cycles were represented in the data. There was still an upward price bias in the equity indices from 2000 through 2013, but that is consistent with the performance of equity indices over most long-term periods.

For each holding period, I calculated the probability advantage of selling OTM options from 0.25 standard deviations (SD) out of the money to 2.0 SD out of the money, in 0.25 SD increments. The probability advantage equals the theoretical (Monte Carlo) probability of touching the strike price of the option sold, minus the realized probability of touching the same strike price.

15

Remember, when selling options, we would prefer that the theoretical probability of touching the short strike price be greater than the realized probability of touching the short strike. When this probability difference (theoretical – actual) was positive, that indicated a historical trading advantage. When this probability difference was negative, this signified a trading disadvantage.

The table of probability advantages for selling OTM *put options* is shown in Figure 1.5 and the table of probability advantages for selling OTM *call options* is presented in Figure 1.6. The historical probability advantage of selling OTM put options was remarkable. I had to run the analysis several times to finally convince myself the results were accurate. Part of the advantage obviously stems from the fact that equity prices have an upward bias, but selling OTM put options on equity indices has a definite trading edge.

Figure 1.5: OTM Short Put Probability Advantage										
#σ/#Days	1	2	3	4	5	6	10	15	20	40	60
0.250	11.80%	8.94%	7.93%	7.22%	7.04%	6.83%	6.75%	6.68%	6.91%	5.84%	5.80%
0.500	9.37%	8.05%	7.12%	6.86%	6.52%	6.64%	6.79%	7.62%	7.83%	7.39%	7.43%
0.750	9.32%	7.71%	7.47%	7.58%	7.79%	7.93%	9.00%	10.36%	10.82%	10.18%	10.10%
1.000	8.38%	7.94%	8.06%	8.71%	8.96%	9.67%	12.41%	13.70%	12.73%	12.01%	11.61%
1.250	8.20%	8.04%	8.55%	9.15%	9.51%	10.38%	12.89%	13.56%	12.82%	12.48%	11.68%
1.500	6.99%	7.35%	7.91%	8.38%	9.11%	9.48%	10.60%	11.05%	10.79%	10.72%	10.11%
1.750	5.36%	5.75%	6.37%	6.85%	7.16%	7.28%	7.80%	8.30%	8.00%	7.60%	7.20%
2.000	3.87%	4.16%	4.43%	4.64%	4.77%	4.77%	5.31%	5.60%	5.39%	4.95%	4.57%

Given the upward price bias in equity indices, it is no surprise that the probability edge from selling OTM call options is not as impressive (Figure 1.6). In fact, for most holding periods, there was a historical disadvantage to selling OTM call options within 0.50 SD from the current price. That disadvantage extended to 0.75 SD for longer holding periods (10 to 60 days).

Figure 1.6 OTM Short Call Probability Advantage										
#σ/#Days	1	2	3	4	5	6	10	15	20	40	60
0.250	8.19%	4.63%	2.32%	1.37%	0.97%	0.06%	-1.66%	-2.19%	-2.75%	-4.36%	-4.86%
0.500	6.21%	3.55%	1.34%	-0.16%	-0.58%	-1.30%	-3.10%	-4.77%	-5.61%	-6.47%	-6.70%
0.750	7.44%	4.17%	2.73%	1.65%	1.44%	0.83%	-0.90%	-2.19%	-3.07%	-3.13%	-3.47%
1.000	7.66%	5.58%	4.61%	4.59%	3.53%	3.21%	2.80%	2.49%	1.91%	1.78%	1.18%
1.250	6.62%	6.04%	5.99%	5.56%	5.26%	4.99%	5.49%	5.53%	5.65%	4.34%	4.04%
1.500	5.59%	5.87%	6.00%	6.19%	5.91%	6.05%	5.83%	5.98%	6.32%	5.91%	5.52%
1.750	4.50%	4.75%	5.25%	5.32%	5.28%	5.35%	5.29%	5.51%	5.48%	5.46%	5.59%
2.000	2.87%	3.30%	3.65%	3.57%	3.72%	3.70%	3.67%	3.96%	4.14%	4.25%	4.21%

Fortunately, the vast majority of holding period/SD pairs demonstrated a significant probability advantage, which provides compelling evidence of an option income strategy trading advantage. The preceding probability data is also invaluable as a guide for identifying, constructing, and managing an option income strategy with a proven historical probability advantage.

Volatility Skews

Before providing one additional piece of evidence supporting the profitability of option income strategies, a brief digression is required. To calculate the probability advantages, I first needed to calculate the OTM strike price for each holding period/SD pair.

Unfortunately, implied volatility is not constant across strike prices or expiration dates. As a result, before calculating the OTM strike prices, I needed to model implied volatility as a function of strike prices (vertical skew) and time-to-expiration (horizontal skew). Again, the volatility model calculations are beyond the scope of this book, but volatility skews are very important when selecting the appropriate strike prices and expiration dates for option income strategies and a brief introduction is required.

The Black-Scholes Option Pricing Model (BSOPM) assumes that volatility is constant, which is obviously not correct. Historically, equity prices fall much more rapidly than they rise. As a result, equity options with lower strike prices have higher implied volatilities and equity options with higher strike prices have lower implied volatilities.

As a result, when attempting to determine the strike price of an OTM call option one SD above the current market price, you would use a lower implied volatility than when calculating the strike price of an OTM put option one SD below the current market price. The resulting plus one SD strike price for the OTM call is closer to the current price than the minus one SD strike price for the OTM put. This is called the vertical skew and it can be modeled.

If you do not regularly use the vertical skew and are more familiar with basic option models that ignore volatility skews, this may seem strange. However, volatility skews are present in the data and should always be incorporated into your risk and return assumptions. Failure to incorporate volatility skews when constructing option strategies is one of the most common mistakes made by option traders. All of the examples in this book incorporate volatility skews, including the construction of option income strategies in later chapters.

Figure 1.7 is OptionVue's graphical depiction of the vertical skew for the May 2013 Russell 2000 Index (RUT) options as of 4/18/2013. OptionVue uses a complex formula to represent the strike prices on the x-axis (horizontal axis). We will not focus on this formula; we only need to recognize that low strike prices are on the left and high strike prices are on the right. In other words, option strike prices increase from left to right on the x-axis.

The implied volatility line in Figure 1.7 is downward sloping, indicating a higher level of implied volatility for RUT options with low strike prices and a lower level of implied volatility for RUT options with high strike prices. The resulting vertical skew exposes the market's implicit assumption that near-term price declines in RUT will be larger and more dramatic than short-term price increases. While the slope and curvature of the vertical skew both change over time, the inverse relationship between strike prices and volatility has persisted in equity index options for many years.

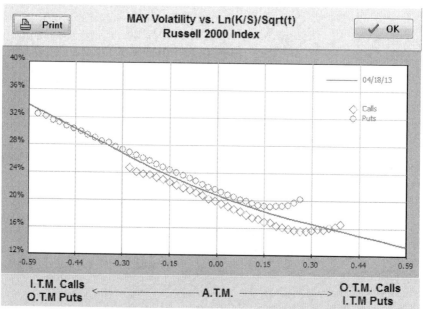

Figure 1.7: OptionVue RUT Vertical Skew Graph

Figure 1.8 illustrates OptionVue's horizontal skew model for RUT on 4/18/2013. I won't go into detail, but a few observations are necessary. First, the implied volatility of near-term options moves more than the implied volatility of long-term options. This relationship can be seen in the shaded volatility cone depicted in the small graph at the top-right corner of the image.

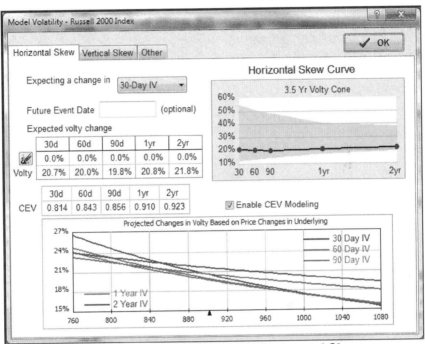

Figure 1.8: OptionVue RUT Horizontal Skew

The other important point is that volatility is assumed to be mean-reverting. When volatility is low (below normal), the term structure of implied volatilities will be upward-sloping. In other words, when volatility is below normal, the market assumes that it will return to normal (increase) over time. In this low volatility environment, longer-dated options will have higher implied volatilities than shorter-dated options.

The opposite is true when volatility is high. When volatility is above normal, the term structure of volatilities will typically be downward sloping; the market assumes that volatility will return to normal over time. In this high volatility environment, longer-dated options will usually have lower implied volatilities than shorter-dated options.

The effects of both the vertical and horizontal skews were incorporated in the calculations of strike prices when determining the probability advantages in Figures 1.5 and 1.6.

One Final Piece of Evidence

Finally, I wanted to provide one additional piece of evidence to support the trading advantage of option income strategies. The theoretical probability advantages are compelling, but they do not represent actual strategy returns. Unfortunately, I cannot take credit for the following insights. They were reported in an article titled "The Variance Premium." The article was written by Euan Sinclair and the article appeared in the February 2013 issue of *Active Trader Magazine*.

In the article, Sinclair tested a simple option income strategy on the QQQ ETF from 2000 to 2010. QQQ is the symbol for a passive ETF that is designed to replicate returns of the NASDAQ 100 index. Sinclair's strategy earned an annual return of 64.1% with a Sharpe ratio (annualized return/risk ratio) of 1.14. Sinclair explains the strategy in detail and even proposes a filter to further improve the results. I strongly encourage you to read the entire article.

In this chapter, I introduced market-neutral option income strategies and provided a wide range of evidence supporting the excess returns available when trading these strategies. Unfortunately, market-neutral strategies often do not stay market-neutral. Before developing the tools necessary to construct and manage option income strategies, we must first review the Greeks, the building blocks of option risk and return calculations.

2 THE GREEKS

In this chapter, we will review each of the option Greeks: Theta, Delta, Gamma, Vega, and Rho. If you have had no prior exposure to this material, you may find it challenging. When I taught courses in financial derivatives, we spent several weeks of class time on these concepts. The best way to master the Greeks is to use them regularly to evaluate a wide range of option strategies. While this book was developed specifically for investors who have some familiarity with options, this chapter includes a complete review of Theta, Delta, Gamma, Vega, and Rho.

The primary purpose of this book is to introduce option strategy risk/return ratios and explain how these new tools can be used to design and manage option income strategies. You will not need to master the Greeks to use these new tools, but a basic knowledge of the Greeks will help you understand how and why these tools work.

We are ultimately interested in the risk and return characteristics of option income strategies, but these types of strategies are complex and are not very intuitive for many traders. We will explore these strategies in great detail in later chapters, but they are not ideally suited for a review of the Greeks. Instead, we will continue to use the same at-the-money call option example that was introduced in Chapter 1.

Most exchange-traded option contracts entitle the buyer of a call or put option to buy or sell 100 shares of the underlying security. However, it is more intuitive to evaluate the Greeks on a per share basis, rather than per 100 shares. As a result, in this chapter, we will assume that each option represents the right to buy or sell only one share of the underlying security. The resulting values will be directly comparable to the price of an option, which is always expressed on a per share basis.

In later chapters, we will use the actual Greek values for each strategy. These values will represent the sum of the Greeks for all long and short positions and will be based on 100 shares per contract.

There are only six basic option positions: long call, short call, long put, short put, long stock, and short stock. These six positions can be combined to form any option strategy. In this book, when a reference is made to a call option or put option with no long or short designation, a long position should be assumed. The table in Figure 2.1 includes a summary of the Greeks for each of the six positions (positive, negative, or zero). You might find it helpful to refer to this table as we review each of the Greeks.

Variable =>	Time	Price	Price	Volatility	Rates
Position	Theta	Delta	Gamma	Vega	Rho
Long Call	-	+	+	+	+
Short Call	+	-	-	-	-
Long Put	-	-	+	+	-
Short Put	+	+	-	-	+
Long Stock	0	+	0	0	0
Short Stock	0	-	0	0	0

Figure 2.1: Greek Summary Table

Theta

Normally, I would begin a presentation of the Greeks by introducing Delta, considered by many to be the most important of the Greeks. However, all market-neutral option income strategies are designed to capitalize on the decay of time value, which is measured by Theta. As a result, Theta is the source of income for option income strategies, so we will begin with Theta.

Theta represents the change in value of an option or option strategy for a one-day decrease in the time remaining until option expiration. Time-to-expiration never increases; it only decreases. As a result, unlike other derivatives, Theta is expressed in terms of a one-day *decrease* in time-to-expiration.

As is the case with the calculation of all of the Greeks, the calculation of Theta assumes that all of the other variables required to determine the value of an option remain unchanged. In other words, the price of the underlying security, the implied volatility, and the risk-free interest rate all remain constant.

For those of you with a mathematics background, you will recognize that Theta and the other Greeks are derivatives; they are derived using stochastic calculus. Fortunately, we do not need to concern ourselves with the derivative formulas. We only need to remember that each of the Greeks estimates the change in one variable for a small change in another variable, holding all other variables constant. Again, Theta estimates the change in the value of an option (or option strategy) for a one day decrease in the time until expiration, holding all other variables constant.

The graph of the at-the-money call option in Figure 2.2 should help make Theta more intuitive. You will remember from the example in Chapter 1 that the kinked payoff or intrinsic value line represents the value of the call option at expiration. The curved line represents the value of the call option today. The stock price is the independent variable and is depicted on the x-axis (horizontal).

If you want to know the sign (positive or negative) of Theta for an option position, you need to ask what happens to the value of the position as we move from the curved current value line to the kinked payoff line. This is exactly what happens to the value of the call option as time passes. As you can see by the downward arrows in Figure 2.2, the Theta of a call option must be negative. The value of the call option will decline as time passes and it moves from the curved current value line toward the kinked payoff line.

In addition to helping us determine the sign of Theta, the graph in Figure 2.2 also provides insight into the relative magnitude of Theta for various prices of the underlying stock. For a deep in-the-money (ITM) call option (stock price much greater than the strike price – at the right side of Figure 2.2), the time value of the option is very small and would suffer minimal decay as time passes. Theta would still be negative, but not nearly as negative as the Theta of an at-the-money (ATM) option. The same is true for options that are far out of the money (stock price much lower than the strike price – at the left side of Figure 2.2). The Theta of an out-of-the-money (OTM) call option would also be negative, but not nearly as negative as the Theta of an at-the-money option.

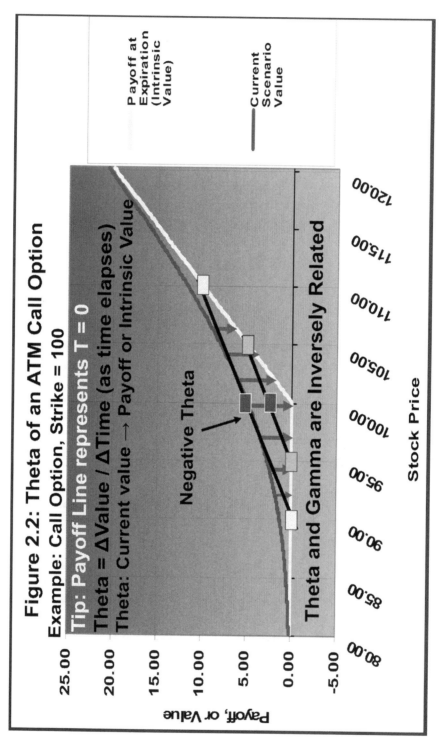

For long option positions, Theta must be negative. Conversely, for short option positions, Theta must be positive. In addition, the magnitude of Theta is greater for ATM options than for ITM or OTM options. Finally, as you will recall from Chapter 1, time value is a function of the square root of time, which means that the time value of short-term options decays at a faster rate than the time value of long-term options (as shown in Figure 1.2). In other words, the *magnitude* of Theta is greater for short-term options than for long-term options. This also means that the magnitude of Theta will increase as time passes, holding all other variables constant. These relationships apply to both call options and put options.

The "income" in option income strategies comes from positive Theta. As a result, all option income strategies are designed to create positive Theta. We can condense all of the Theta relationships into three principles for creating market-neutral option income strategies:

1. Sell near-the-money options and buy options that are further out of the money.

2. Sell short-term options and buy longer-term options.

3. For every option sold, buy an option of the same type (call or put) to limit risk and reduce required capital.

Delta

While Theta represents a source of income or return for market-neutral option income strategies, the other Greeks represent a source of risk. Remember, market-neutral means that we would like to construct strategies that have no directional bias. Ideally we would like to create an option income strategy with positive Theta, while constraining all of the other Greeks to be equal to zero. If this were possible, the value of the strategy would increase over time and it would have no risk. This would be called a riskless arbitrage. Certain types of riskless arbitrage do exist for very brief periods. Unfortunately, it is mathematically impossible to create an option strategy with positive Theta and zero values for the other Greeks.

Nevertheless, attempting to maximize return (Theta) and minimize risk (Delta, Gamma, Vega, and Rho) would be excellent objectives when constructing market-neutral option income strategies. This insight was the inspiration for the new option risk/return ratios that will be presented in Chapters 4, 5, and 6. For now, let's continue our review of the Greeks that are the sources of risk for option income strategies.

Figure 2.3 is the now familiar graph of the kinked payoff line and curved current value line of a hypothetical call option with a strike price of $100, plotted against the price of the underlying stock. As we would expect, the value of the call option increases in response to an increase in the underlying stock price. However, for an at-the-money call option, the value of the call option will not change on a dollar-for-dollar basis with the price of the underlying stock.

The change in the value of the option for a $1 increase in the price of the underlying stock is called Delta. It is the slope of the curved line in Figure 2.3 (actually, it is the slope $[\Delta y/\Delta x]$ of the straight tangent line that intersects the curved current value line at the current stock price of $100). Delta is one of the most important and often used risk measures in options management and trading. It is the primary measure of market risk.

A positive Delta represents a bullish position – one that benefits from an increase in the price of the underlying security. A negative Delta represents a bearish position – one that benefits from a decrease in the price of the underlying security. A Delta of zero (or close to zero) represents a neutral position, which is our aim when creating market-neutral option income strategies.

For call options, Delta will always be between zero and one. It cannot be negative. When the stock price is approximately equal to the strike price of $100, as shown in Figure 2.3, Delta will be approximately 0.5. This means that the price of the at-the-money call option would increase by about $0.50 for a $1.00 increase in the price of the underlying stock.

Remember, the value of an option equals the probability-weighted future payoff values (discounted back to the present). For an at-the-money call option, the probability of expiring in the money would only be about 50%. As a result, a $1 increase in the price of the underlying stock would only increase the price of the call option by about $0.50.

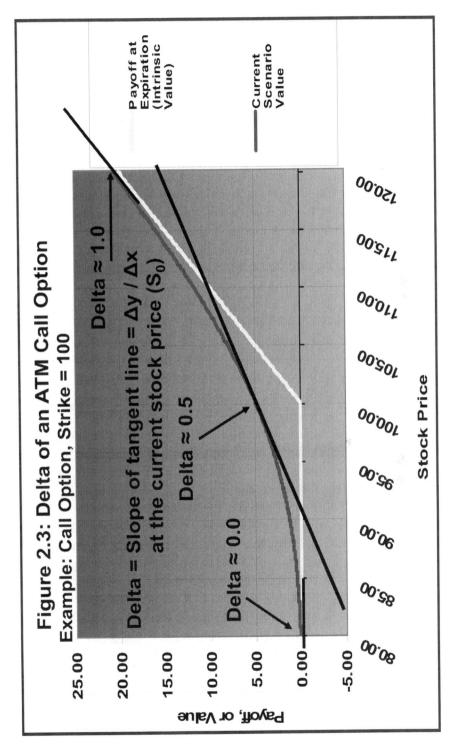

Figure 2.3: Delta of an ATM Call Option
Example: Call Option, Strike = 100

Delta ≈ 1.0

Delta = Slope of tangent line = Δy / Δx at the current stock price (S_0)

Delta ≈ 0.5

Delta ≈ 0.0

Payoff at Expiration (Intrinsic Value)

Current Scenario Value

Payoff, or Value

Stock Price

As the price of the underlying stock rises further above the strike price, the Delta of the call option would increase gradually and would eventually approach 1.0 (the slope of the payoff function for in-the-money call options). At a price of $120 on the underlying stock, the probability of the stock being in the money at expiration (stock price > $100) would be almost 100%. As a result, at a stock price of $120, the value of the option would increase almost dollar for dollar with the underlying stock. At a price of $120, notice that the slope of the curved, current value line is approaching the slope of the kinked, payoff line (+ 1.0).

Conversely, as the stock price falls far below the strike price (out of the money), the resulting Delta (or slope of the tangent line) would eventually approach zero (the slope of the payoff line for out-of-the money call options). At a price of $80 on the underlying stock, the probability of the stock being in the money at expiration (stock price > $100) would approach 0%. As a result, at a stock price of $80, the value of the option would only increase by pennies for a $1 increase in the price of the stock. At a price of $80, notice that the slope of the curved current value line is nearing the slope of the kinked payoff line (0.0).

When constructing market-neutral option income strategies, Delta should initially be as close to zero as possible, subject to the availability of options with the desired strike prices and expiration dates. Delta represents market risk. If Delta is not approximately zero, then the option income strategy is not market-neutral.

Unfortunately, as explained earlier, changes in the price of the underlying security cause Delta to change as well. To understand how, let's return briefly to the earlier call option example. When the price of the underlying security increases, Delta also increases. In other words, as prices rise, a call option automatically becomes more bullish. When the price of the underlying security falls, Delta also declines. In this scenario, the call option becomes less bullish. This is great for the owner of the call option, but is not so great for the seller of the option. Changes in Delta always hurt option sellers and this creates significant challenges for all option income strategies.

Gamma

Figure 2.4 is another depiction of the call option example we have used throughout this book. You will notice that the current value line is not straight; it is curved. As explained earlier, Delta changes in response to movements in the underlying stock price. Gamma is a measure of the degree of curvature of the current value line. It represents the change in Delta (or slope) for a one dollar increase in the price of the underlying stock.

Intuitively, if the curved line were above the straight tangent line, then Gamma would be positive, as it is for the at-the-money call option. If the curved current value line were below the straight tangent line, then Gamma would be negative. The straight line represents a linear estimate of the price of the option at various prices of the underlying stock. The linear estimates were derived using the Delta of the at-the-money call option (0.50), which was calculated at the current stock price of $100.

As you can see in Figure 2.4, the call option will perform better than the linear estimate (Delta), if the price of the underlying stock moves up or moves down. In other words, the curved current value line is above the straight line at all points. This means that Gamma is positive; the change in Delta (as a function of the price change in the underlying stock) will always help a long call option. The larger the price change, the more Gamma would help the position. The effect of Gamma on the value of the position is exponential, not linear.

For the at-the-money call option in Figure 2.4, Delta increases as the price of the underlying stock rises. In other words, in a rising market, the option value would increase at a faster rate than implied by the initial value of Delta. Similarly, Delta would decrease as the price of the underlying stock drops. In other words, in a declining market, the option value would decrease at a slower rate than implied by the initial value of Delta.

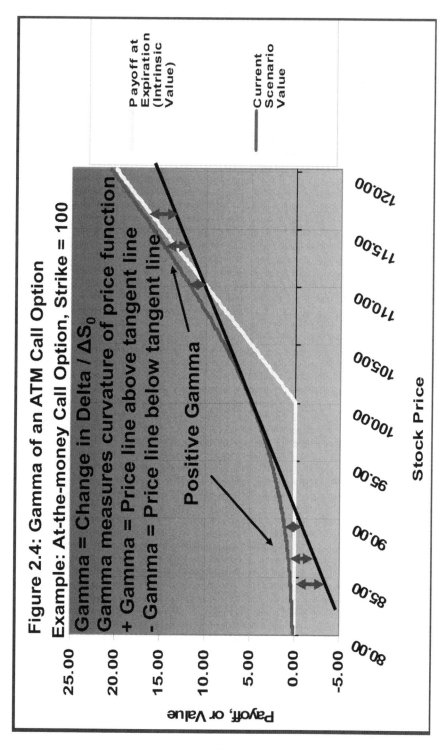

Figure 2.4: Gamma of an ATM Call Option

Example: At-the-money Call Option, Strike = 100

Gamma = Change in Delta / ΔS_0

Gamma measures curvature of price function

+ Gamma = Price line above tangent line

- Gamma = Price line below tangent line

Positive Gamma

For long option positions (calls or puts), Gamma is always positive. For short option positions, Gamma is always negative. You will also notice that the current value line is more curved when the price of the underlying stock is near the strike price. The magnitude of Gamma is greater for at-the-money options than for in-the-money or out-of-the money options.

This makes sense; the value of asymmetry is higher when the price of the underlying stock is near the strike price. You will recall that asymmetry explains why the magnitude of Theta is also higher for at-the-money options. As a result, selling near-the-money options and buying out-of-the money options to create positive Theta will also produce negative Gamma.

Theta and Gamma represent the costs and benefits of asymmetry. Unfortunately, that means when Theta is positive, Gamma is negative. Negative Gamma represents the cost of positive Theta. Said differently, Theta represents our compensation for incurring the adverse symmetry of negative Gamma.

Option income strategies always have positive Theta (or they would not be income strategies), which guarantees that option income strategies always have negative Gamma. As a result, Delta-neutral option income strategies do not remain Delta-neutral. Significant changes in the price of the underlying security will cause material changes in Delta. To make matters worse, when this happens, Theta typically decreases as well. As a result, price changes increase the risk and reduce the potential return of option income strategies. The increased risk and reduced return can force us to either adjust (execute transactions to reduce risk) or close our option income strategies.

Just as price changes in the underlying security affect the risk and return characteristics of option income strategies, the passage of time can also create challenges. The magnitude of Theta and Gamma both increase over time, which improves potential returns, but also magnifies risk. As time passes and option expiration approaches, the risk of option income strategies can change very rapidly.

How you evaluate and manage your option income strategies, as their risk and return characteristics change, will determine the success or failure of your strategy. The risk/return ratios presented in the following chapters will provide you with the framework and tools necessary to make these decisions objectively and consistently for any option income strategy.

Vega

Vega, like Delta, is a measure of market risk, which means that we would like to minimize Vega in our market-neutral option income strategies. While Delta measures the risk of a change in the price of the underlying stock price, Vega measures the risk of a change in implied volatility. Specifically, Vega measures the change in the value of an option or option strategy for a 1% increase in the annual implied volatility (also called sigma or the standard deviation) of the expected future returns of the underlying stock.

Investors who are long options benefit from increases in implied volatility. Investors who are short options are harmed by increases in implied volatility. This is due to the asymmetry of option payoff functions, which was covered in Chapter 1. When implied volatility (the expected future level of volatility) increases, the value of asymmetry increases, which translates to higher option prices. As a result, greater expected or implied volatility is good for option holders (buyers) and bad for option writers (sellers).

The graph of our standard long call option in Figure 2.5 can provide some intuition regarding the sign or direction of Vega, but there is a trick to using the graph when analyzing Vega. Normally, when we think of the payoff line, we assume that time until expiration equals zero. However, if volatility equals zero, then the price today must also be the price at expiration (with zero volatility, prices cannot change), even if there is time remaining until expiration. As a result, we can also use the payoff line to represent sigma or implied volatility equal to zero. We can now use the relationship between the current value line and the payoff line (sigma = 0) to determine the direction or sign of Vega.

Vega measures the change in the value of the option for a 1% *increase* in sigma (annual implied volatility). If sigma were to *decrease*, we would move from the curved current value line toward the kinked payoff line (sigma = 0). However, Vega measures the effect of an increase in sigma, so we want to know what happens to the value of the call option when the curved line (current option value) moves *away* from the kinked payoff line (sigma = 0). This is depicted by the upward arrows in Figure 2.5.

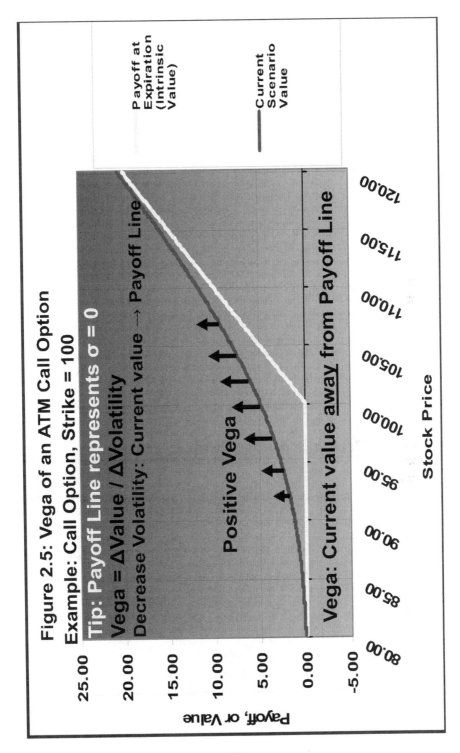

Figure 2.5: Vega of an ATM Call Option

Example: Call Option, Strike = 100

Tip: Payoff Line represents σ = 0

Vega = ΔValue / ΔVolatility

Decrease Volatility: Current value → Payoff Line

Positive Vega

Vega: Current value away from Payoff Line

Payoff at Expiration (Intrinsic Value)

Current Scenario Value

Stock Price

Payoff, or Value

25.00
20.00
15.00
10.00
5.00
0.00
-5.00

80.00
85.00
90.00
95.00
100.00
105.00
110.00
115.00
120.00

As sigma increases, the current value of the call option will move away from the payoff line and increase in value. This means that the Vega of the call option is positive. In fact, the Vega of any long option position is positive.

If the Vega chart is not intuitive, think about the value of asymmetry when volatility increases. Since the option buyer decides whether to exercise the option, asymmetry always benefits the option buyer. An increase in the expected level of future volatility would increase the probability weighted payoffs for both call and put options, which would result in higher option values.

As we saw with Gamma and Theta, the magnitude of Vega is also greater for at-the-money options than for in-the-money or out-of-the money options. Again, this is due to the increased importance of asymmetry and volatility when the price of the underlying stock is near the strike price.

Vega is also related to the time-to-expiration of the option. For options with more time remaining until expiration, an increase in the annualized expected level of future volatility will have a larger impact. As a result, Vega is an increasing function of time remaining until expiration. As you will recall from our analysis of time decay, price dispersion is assumed to be a function of the square root of time, not of time itself.

Figure 2.6 is a graph of Vega for an at-the-money (ATM) call option and an ATM put option (dotted line) as a function of time. The Vega of a call option will always equal the Vega of a put option with the same strike price and time-to-expiration. Time-to-expiration is depicted on the x-axis (horizontal) and the Vega of the ATM call option relates to the left-hand y-axis (vertical).

Finally, the solid line (lower) represents the square root of the number of days until expiration and these values correspond to the right-hand y-axis (vertical). As you can see from the graph, Vega is clearly a function of the square root of time remaining until expiration.

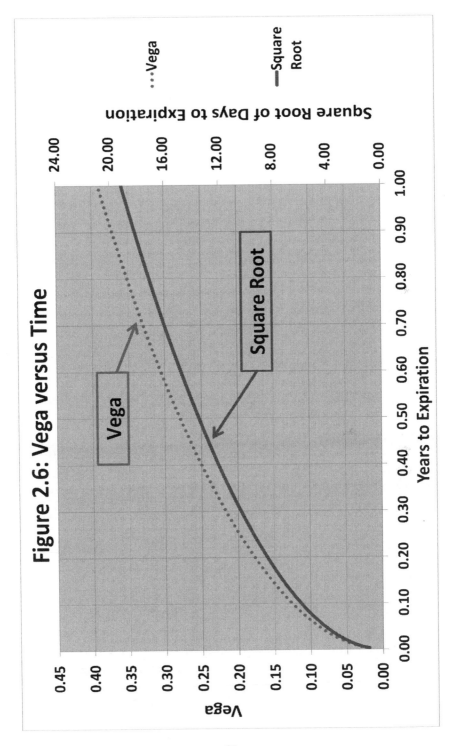

Figure 2.6: Vega versus Time

So what are the implications for market-neutral option income strategies? Vega risk is a form of market risk and should be eliminated or at least minimized. Let's revisit the three principles for creating market-neutral option income strategies that were introduced earlier in this chapter and examine the implications for Vega:

1. Sell near-the-money options and buy options that are further out of the money.

2. Sell short-term options and buy longer-term options.

3. For every option sold, buy an option of the same type to limit risk and reduce required capital.

The first rule involves selling near-the-money options and buying options that are further out of the money. Recall that the magnitude of Vega is greater for ATM options than for ITM or OTM options. As a result, selling near-the-money options and buying OTM options will generate negative Vega. The resulting income strategy would have negative Vega and would be adversely exposed to an increase in implied volatility. Condors (Chapter 7) and butterflies (Chapter 9) use this approach to generate positive Theta and both strategies have negative Vega.

The second method for creating positive Theta involves selling short-term options and buying longer-term options. Vega of longer-term options is greater than Vega of shorter-term options (Figure 2.6). As a result, selling near-term options and buying longer-term options will produce positive Vega. Using this approach to create positive Theta would result in option income strategies with positive Vega that would be adversely exposed to a decrease in implied volatility. Calendar or time-spreads (Chapter 8) use this approach to generate positive Theta and have positive Vega.

Unfortunately, condor, butterfly, and calendar spreads have either negative or positive Vega by construction. Therefore, these types of option income strategies are not market-neutral, even when these strategies are initiated.

Could we create an option income strategy with minimal Vega risk? Fortunately, the answer is yes. The two methods for creating positive Theta generate negative and positive Vega, respectively. If we combined the two methods described earlier, we could create an option income strategy with minimal exposure to Delta or Vega and reasonable exposure to Gamma.

The resulting strategy would be approximately market-neutral with respect to the price of the underlying security *and* with respect to changes in implied volatility. Double diagonals (Chapter 10) and hybrid combinations (Chapter 11) use this technique to reduce, but not completely eliminate Vega exposure.

Rho

Finally, the least intuitive of the Greeks is Rho. Rho represents the change in the value of an option for a 1% increase in the risk-free rate of interest. When valuing options using standard option pricing models like the Black-Scholes Option Pricing Model, U.S. Treasury rates are often used as a proxy for the risk-free interest rate. The U.S. Treasury instrument with a maturity date closest to the expiration date of the option should be used. For example, the yield of a three-month T-Bill would be used to value an option with three months remaining until expiration.

Options are similar to levered positions in the underlying stock. A call option is similar to a long position in the underlying stock, funded by borrowing money at the risk-free rate of interest. A put option is similar to a short position in the underlying stock, with the proceeds of the short sale invested at the risk-free interest rate. Given that changes in interest rates affect the value of debt instruments (borrowing or lending), a change in the risk-free rate will affect the value of both call and put options; Rho is used to quantify this risk.

Rho measures the effect of changes in the rate of interest on the degree of borrowing or lending that is implicit in the structure of call and put options. If you are not familiar with the effects of changing interest rates on debt instruments, Rho will not be very intuitive. However, it is still possible to gain some understanding into Rho by graphing Rho versus time.

Figure 2.7 is a graph of Rho for ATM call options (dotted line) and ATM put options (dashed line) as a function of time. Time-to-expiration is depicted on the x-axis (horizontal) and the values of Rho for the call and put options are plotted on the left-hand y-axis (vertical).

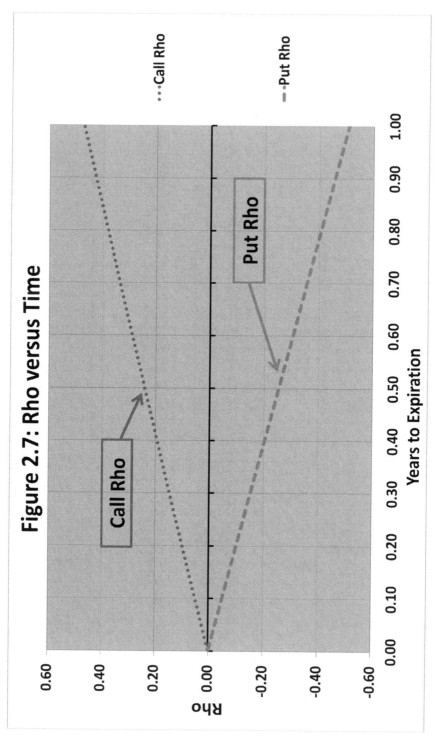

Figure 2.7: Rho versus Time

The most obvious observation is that Rho is positive for call options and negative for put options. However, these values do not exactly offset. In addition, the magnitude of Rho for both calls and puts is an increasing function of time, but the relationship is almost linear. Unlike several of the relationships discussed earlier, Rho is not a function of the square root of time.

Rho is also related to the price of the underlying security. This relationship requires some thought. Figure 2.8 is a graph of Rho for one-year ATM call options (dotted line) and one-year ATM put options (dashed line) as a function of the price of the underlying security. Both options have strike prices of $100, which is in the center of the graph. The price of the underlying stock is depicted on the x-axis (horizontal) and the values of Rho for the call and put options are plotted on the left-hand y-axis (vertical).

Interest rate changes have the greatest effect on in-the-money options, less effect on at-the-money options, and very little effect on out-of-the-money options. As a result, the magnitude of Rho will be much higher for ITM options than for OTM options.

The call options in Figure 2.8 would be in the money when the price of the underlying stock was above the $100 strike price and out of the money when the price of the underlying stock was below the $100 strike price. As a result, OTM values for call options are on the left side of the chart and ITM values for call options are on the right side of the chart. As explained earlier, the magnitude of Rho is higher for ITM options than for OTM options. This is consistent with the values of Rho for call options in the chart that increase from left to right (OTM to ITM).

Conversely, the put options in Figure 2.8 would be in the money when the price of the underlying stock was below the $100 strike price and out of the money when the price of the underlying stock was above the $100 strike price.

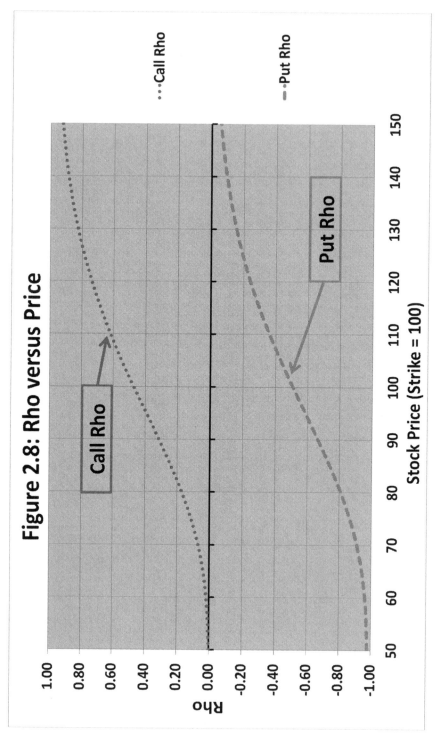

As a result, OTM values for put options are on the right side of the chart and ITM values for put options are on the left side of the chart. As explained earlier, the magnitude of Rho is higher for ITM options than for OTM options. This is consistent with the values of Rho in the chart. The magnitude of the values of Rho for put options increases from right to left (OTM to ITM). In other words, the values of Rho become more negative as put options move from out of the money to in the money.

As was the case with Delta, Gamma, and Vega, Rho represents risk to option income strategies. However, as noted earlier, U.S. Treasury rates have been near zero for several years (2008-2014). As a result, there has been very little change in the level of rates during this period and many traders ignore Rho. Nevertheless, rates will not be near zero forever and there has been substantial volatility in rates in the past. As a result, I included Rho in this chapter and I also created a specific risk/return ratio for Rho in Chapter 6.

Theta represents the source of income or return for option income strategies. Delta, Gamma, Vega, and Rho represent risk for option income strategies and all of these risks should be minimized. As explained in this chapter, despite our best intentions, Greek values change as a function of time, price, and volatility. When the Greeks change, the risk and return characteristics of option income strategies also change.

In the next chapter, we will briefly review some of the common heuristics used by market practitioners to manage option income strategies as their characteristics change. This will help us identify desirable attributes for strategy management metrics and complete the foundation for the introduction of risk/return ratios in Chapters 4, 5, and 6.

3 OPTION STRATEGY HEURISTICS

Market-neutral option income strategies are complex, and many option traders have leveraged their prior experience to develop a number of simple rules-of-thumb or heuristics to manage these types of strategies. We will examine several of the most common approaches in this chapter. However, before we can proceed, we need to develop a set of desirable attributes or criteria. These criteria will not only be used to evaluate existing heuristics, they will also provide a roadmap for the development of option strategy risk/return ratios in the subsequent chapters.

Ideally, tools used to create and manage market-neutral option income strategies would:

1. be applicable to all market-neutral option income strategies,
2. be suitable for creating "optimal" option income strategies,
3. facilitate the establishment of objective entry, exit, and adjustment rules,
4. include elements of both risk and return in the same measure or metric,
5. provide a numerical value or values that would allow meaningful comparisons across time and among different strategies, and
6. incorporate the unique characteristics of the specific market environment in the calculation of risk and return.

The first three items in the list are general criteria that will allow us to effectively and efficiently manage our option income strategies. Items 4-6 are specific conditions that will help us identify or create tools to accomplish the three broad objectives.

Our primary objective is to allocate our capital to option income strategies that offer the highest rate of return per unit of risk, or the lowest level of risk per unit of return. In other words, we would prefer to allocate our investment capital to option income strategies

42

that offer the highest risk-adjusted returns.

To identify the best or optimal strategy at any given time, we would need to evaluate all prospective market-neutral strategies. Given the countless number of possible strategies, strikes, and expiration dates, it would be even more efficient to use a set of statistics to create the best strategy – one that offers the highest risk-adjusted return.

However, as explained in Chapter 2, risk and return characteristics change continuously as a function of price, volatility, and time. Even if we were able to identify the best strategy, we would still need to determine the best time to adjust or exit that strategy.

To identify the best risk-adjusted strategy, our tools must incorporate elements of both risk and return. We cannot simply maximize return, while ignoring the effect on risk. In order to identify the best strategy among a wide range of alternatives, specific numerical values are required and those values must be comparable across time and among different strategies. As the risk and return characteristics of our strategies change, we must be able to quantify those changes.

Finally, our tools also need to incorporate the unique characteristics of the specific market environment in the calculation of risk and return. The Greeks are invaluable, but they measure risk per a stated unit of change, and that unit of change is unrelated to the actual market environment. As a result, standard Greek-based heuristics overstate risk in low volatility environments and understate risk in high volatility environments. We can now use these criteria to examine several common option income strategy heuristics.

Negative Theta Rule

One of the most logical option income strategy rules is Theta must always be positive. We would obviously never enter an option income position that has negative Theta. However, if the price of the underlying security moved enough, Theta would eventually become negative. If this happened, the negative Theta rules would require that the strategy be adjusted or liquidated.

As far as this rule goes, it does offer sound advice. If the position has negative Theta, it would no longer be an option income strategy and the reason for entering the trade would no longer be valid.

Unfortunately, if Theta turns negative, the option income trade would probably be under water. In other words, liquidating the position would result in a realized loss.

To make matters worse, the risk due to Delta and Gamma would probably have increased as well. Unfortunately, traders who do not have objective exit rules often fail to liquidate their option income strategies in this situation. Instead of cutting their losses, they hope that the price trend will reverse, which would reduce their losses. This is equivalent to making a directional bet, with time (negative Theta) working against them.

While the negative Theta Rule would definitely help undisciplined traders, it does not meet all of our criteria. On the plus side, it is applicable to all option income strategies. Unfortunately, it would not help us create optimal strategies, because it does not include elements of both risk and return.

Theta represents the prospective return for option income strategies, but the negative Theta rule does not directly measure risk. At the point where Theta turns negative, the amount of risk would be different for every strategy. As a result, the negative Theta rule would not help us manage risk consistently. Finally, the negative Theta rule does not allow us to compare strategies nor does it incorporate the characteristics of the specific market environment. It falls well short of meeting our requirements.

Expiration Breakeven Rule

The expiration breakeven rule is very similar to the negative Theta rule and it suffers from the same flaws. The expiration breakeven rule states that the strategy must be liquidated or adjusted when the price of the underlying security moves beyond the expiration breakeven price.

What is the expiration breakeven price? Option income strategies all have positive Theta and negative Gamma. This means that they do well when the price of the underlying security stays the same or moves less than expected. Using an option model, we can estimate the value of the option income strategy at the expiration date of the nearest-dated option and compare that value to the initial value of the strategy. When the value of the strategy at expiration exactly equals the initial value of the strategy, this would represent a breakeven price. Since most option income strategies are somewhat symmetric, there will typically be two expiration breakeven prices, one for an increase in the price of the underlying security and one for a decrease in the price of the underlying security.

If the price of the underlying security moved beyond one of the expiration breakeven values, we would be forced to liquidate or adjust our strategy. Some traders add or subtract an arbitrary percentage amount to the breakeven values, but the process is the same. The expiration breakeven rule assumes that when the price of the underlying security reaches an expiration breakeven point, or some nearby value, the strategy would no longer be attractive.

As was the case with the negative Theta rule, the expiration breakeven rule would provide an objective rule for exiting positions and it is applicable to all option income strategies. Unfortunately, it would not help us create optimal strategies, because it does not include elements of both risk and return. The expiration breakeven rule does not directly measure risk or return.

In addition, at the expiration breakeven prices, the amount of risk would be different for every strategy. Furthermore, for strategies with multiple option expiration dates, the expiration breakeven prices would change continuously as a function of implied volatility. This would turn the expiration breakeven prices into moving targets, which would make the rule almost impossible to apply in practice. The rule could be applied to some strategies (butterflies and condors), but not to others (calendars and double diagonals), which would controvert our objectives.

The expiration breakeven rule does not facilitate the comparison of strategies nor does it incorporate the unique characteristics of the specific market environment. It fails to satisfy many of our criteria.

Delta/Theta

Some option traders have taken a more sophisticated approach to heuristics and created a ratio of two Greek values. This technique is insightful and represents a step in the right direction. Option income strategies are designed to be market neutral. As a result, Delta represents a source of risk. As the magnitude of Delta increases (positively or negatively), the risk of an option income strategy also increases. Theta represents a source of return. As Theta increases, the prospective return of an option income strategy also increases. Therefore, the Delta/Theta ratio represents a risk/return ratio, which we would like to minimize.

We could lower the Delta/Theta ratio by reducing the magnitude of Delta, by increasing the value of Theta, or by doing a combination of both. The Delta/Theta ratio will also automatically capture changes in the risk and return characteristics of a strategy as prices change. As explained in an earlier example, large price movements will cause the magnitude of Delta to increase and Theta to decrease for most option income strategies. The large move in price would cause the numerator (risk) of the Delta/Theta ratio to increase and the denominator (return) of the Delta/Theta ratio to decrease. The resulting value of the Delta/Theta ratio would increase significantly, accurately reflecting the increase in risk per unit of return.

So far, the Delta/Theta ratio seems promising. It is applicable to all option income strategies; it could be used to optimize strategies and to establish objective entry, exit, and adjustment rules. It even combines elements of risk and return in the same ratio and adjusts continuously as the market moves.

Unfortunately, there are some significant problems with the Delta/Theta ratio. It is designed to relate the price risk of an option income strategy to the prospective return; however, Delta is only one component of price risk. It is easy to eliminate Delta risk, but Gamma represents the main source of price risk for option income strategies and Gamma risk cannot be eliminated. As a result, Gamma risk must be quantified and included in any statistic that endeavors to measure price risk.

Delta/Theta ratios are numerical values, but those values are not comparable across time or across different underlying instruments. In addition, the Delta/Theta ratio does not incorporate the specific market environment in the risk and return calculations. However, the reason may not be immediately obvious.

Delta represents the change in the value of the strategy for a one dollar increase in the price of the underlying security. Theta represents the change in the value of the strategy for a one day decrease in the time-to-expiration. Regardless of the market environment, time-to-expiration will decrease by one day, every day. Regrettably, the likelihood of a one dollar increase in the price of the underlying security is not constant. Not only is it dependent on the price of the underlying security, it is highly dependent on the volatility environment, which can change dramatically over time.

Underlying securities with higher prices and higher expected volatilities have higher expected price changes. Underlying securities with lower price and lower expected volatilities have lower expected price changes. Unfortunately, the same underlying security can have drastically different implied volatilities over time.

To demonstrate this, we can use the VIX Index as a proxy for the implied volatility of 30-day S&P 500 Index (SPX) options. From 2008 through 2013, the closing values of the VIX Index ranged from a low of 9.00% in early 2013 to a high of 79.10% in late 2008. The highest level of implied volatility was more than eight times the lowest level of implied volatility – for the same underlying security (SPX). This means the expected percentage price change of SPX in 2008 was more than eight times the expected percentage price change of SPX in early 2013.

If an option income strategy had identical Delta/Theta ratios in 2008 and 2013, would the ratios be comparable? Of course not, even after adjusting for the different price levels of SPX, the expected price change in 2008 would have been much higher than the expected price change in 2013. Due to the high volatility environment, the option income strategy in 2008 would have been much riskier, even though it had the same Delta/Theta ratio as the strategy in 2013.

Delta represents the change in the value of an option strategy for a one dollar increase in the price of the underlying security, but the expected price change in the underlying security would have been much greater in 2008 than in 2013. The Delta/Theta ratio is a step in the right direction, but it does not incorporate the effects of Gamma and it fails to meet our last two criteria (comparability & market specific).

Vega/Theta

Delta and Gamma both measure price risk and should be combined in the same risk/return measure; Vega risk is separate from price risk and therefore warrants its own metric. Option traders have attempted to relate volatility risk to return potential by calculating the Vega/Theta ratio. The concept is very similar to the Delta/Theta ratio.

While Delta measures the risk of a change in the price of the underlying security, Vega measures the risk of a change in implied volatility. As explained in Chapter 2, Vega measures the change in the value of an option for a 1% increase in the annualized implied volatility (also called sigma or the standard deviation) of the expected future returns of the underlying security.

Vega represents a source of risk. As the magnitude of Vega increases (positively or negatively), the risk of an option income strategy also increases. Theta represents a source of return. As Theta increases, the prospective return of an option income strategy also increases. Therefore, the Vega/Theta ratio represents a risk/return ratio, which we would like to minimize.

We could lower the Vega/Theta ratio by reducing the magnitude of Vega, by increasing the value of Theta, or by doing a combination of both. The Vega/Theta ratio will also automatically capture changes in the risk and return characteristics of an option income strategy as prices and volatility change.

The Vega/Theta ratio is applicable to all option income strategies and it could be used to optimize strategies and to establish objective entry, exit, and adjustment rules. It combines elements of risk and return in the same ratio and adjusts continuously as the market moves.

When evaluating the Delta/Theta ratio earlier, I stressed the importance of including Gamma (the curvature or convexity of the price function) when measuring price risk. There is a corresponding Greek called Vomma that measures the convexity of Vega, just as Gamma measures the convexity of Delta. However, the rate of change in Vega (Vomma) is not nearly as significant as the rate of change in Delta (Gamma). In addition, Vomma is not typically available on most option analytical platforms. As a result, excluding Vomma from the volatility risk calculation would be justified, but excluding Gamma would not be.

Unfortunately, as was the case with Delta/Theta ratios, Vega/Theta ratios are not comparable across time or across different underlying instruments. Vega/Theta ratios do not incorporate the specific market environment in the calculation of risk.

Vega represents the change in the value of an option strategy for a 1% increase in implied volatility. However, the likelihood of a 1%

increase in the implied volatility is not constant. The magnitude of the expected change in implied volatility is highly dependent on the volatility environment, which changes materially over time.

We explored high and low volatility environments by examining the range of the VIX Index from 2008 through 2013. During this period, the closing values of the VIX Index ranged from a low of 9.00% in early 2013 to a high of 79.10% in late 2008. The likelihood of a 1% change in volatility would have been much greater in 2008 when the VIX was 79.1% than in 2013 when the VIX was only 9.0%. As a result, the Vega/Theta ratio understates risk in high volatility environments (2008) and overstates risk in low volatility environments (2013).

The Greek ratios are insightful, but we need risk/return ratios that provide consistent measures of risk and return across all underlying securities in all market environments.

4 DELTA/THETA RISK/RETURN RATIO (DTRRR)

The risk/return ratios that will be presented in Chapters 4, 5, and 6 were designed to overcome the deficiencies of the common heuristics and to meet all of the criteria outlined in Chapter 3. The risk/return formulas in the next three chapters are relatively straightforward and only require basic algebra.

In addition to providing the general formulas, numerical examples will also be presented. All of the remaining examples used in this book use specific values as of the close on April 18, 2013. The initial values and intermediate calculations were rounded for presentation purposes, but the final calculations reflect the full level of precision available in Excel.

The risk/return ratios in Chapters 4, 5, and 6 were calculated on the assumed entry date for an iron condor strategy, which we will examine in greater detail in Chapter 7. For now, an iron condor strategy is a market-neutral option income strategy that requires selling an OTM put credit spread and an OTM call credit spread. The underlying security used in all of these calculations was the Russell 2000 Index (RUT). The required capital for all strategy examples was between $5,000 and $10,000.

Reviewing the formulas and examples in the next few chapters will help you understand the rationale behind the risk/return ratios, which should prove invaluable when you apply them in practice. However, you will not need to do these calculations manually. I created an Excel spreadsheet that contains several macros that will do all of the required risk/return calculations. Simply enter the Greeks for your strategy and some market-specific data and the macros will perform all of the calculations for you. The Resources section in the back of this book will explain how to download the Excel spreadsheet.

For those of you who would like to work with the formulas directly, all of the requisite formulas will be provided in the next three chapters. The formulas will be presented in Excel format, which should facilitate the creation of your own Excel spreadsheets.

DTRRR

The Delta/Theta Risk/Return Ratio (DTRRR) represents the expected loss (risk) incurred by an option income strategy due to an adverse price change in the underlying security, divided by the expected gain (return) earned if the price of the underlying security remained constant.

By definition, the value of this ratio will always be negative for option income strategies. As explained earlier, all option income strategies have positive Theta, or they would not be income strategies. Consequently, the passage of time will result in a gain for option income strategies – assuming all other variables (price, implied volatility, and interest rates) remain constant. Accordingly, the DTRRR denominator, which represents prospective return, will always be positive.

Positive Theta represents the compensation for incurring the risk of negative Gamma. Therefore, every option strategy with positive Theta will also have negative Gamma. This guarantees that an instantaneous adverse price change will always generate a loss for an option income strategy. Hence, the DTRRR numerator, which represents risk, will always be negative.

We would like to reduce the magnitude of risk (the numerator) and increase return (the denominator); therefore, we would like the magnitude of the DTRRR to be as small a negative number as possible, which would reflect a low level of price risk per unit of return.

So, how do we calculate the expected gain from the passage of time and the expected loss due to an adverse price change?

DTRRR Formulas & Sample Calculations

The calculation of the expected gain from the passage of time is straightforward. Theta denotes the change in the value of an option strategy as a function of time. Specifically, Theta equals the daily change in the value of an option strategy, holding all other variables constant. So, if we wanted to determine the expected gain from the passage of time over three calendar days, we would simply multiply Theta by three. We will explore the effect of the choice of holding period on the DTRRR later in this chapter. The general formulas that follow will work for any number of days, but the examples and calculations used throughout this book assume a holding period of three calendar days.

HPD = Number of Calendar Days in Holding Period
Theta Effect (TE) = Theta * HPD
Theta Effect (TE) = \$29.26 * 3 = \$87.78
Theta Effect (TE) = \$87.78

The prospective gain from holding the iron condor strategy over three calendar days was \$87.78, assuming all other variables remained constant. Obviously, this formula only approximates the actual gain. This calculation assumes that all other variables remain constant and that Theta is constant over time. Both of these assumptions will be violated in practice, but our objective is to create a practical risk/return measure, not to forecast the precise gain or loss to the penny.

The calculation of the expected loss from an adverse change in price is more complicated. As demonstrated in Chapter 3, Delta and Gamma both contribute to price risk and the effects of both Greeks must be included in the estimated loss calculation. In addition, we also noted that price risk must incorporate the market-specific effects of price level and volatility, both of which influence the magnitude of expected price changes in the underlying security.

Given that the DTRRR includes the effects of both Delta and Gamma, why is it called the Delta/Theta Risk/Return Ratio? Because Gamma measures the change in Delta as a function of price, so Gamma is really a non-linear form of Delta risk.

Before we can calculate the Delta and Gamma Effects and their combined contribution to the price risk of the iron condor strategy, we must first calculate the expected change in the price of the underlying security (RUT), over the same three calendar-day period that we used in the calculation of the Theta Effect.

The expected change in the price of an underlying security is a function of the price of the underlying security, the length of the holding period, and the expected level of volatility. The good news is that we know all three values. The price of the underlying security changes continuously, but is directly observable in real-time. We are assuming a three-day holding period for all risk/return ratio calculations.

Finally, while we do not know the actual level of price volatility that will be realized over the next three calendar days, we do know the market's estimate of the expected level of volatility. You will recall that this value is called the implied volatility of an option and if you have access to real-time option prices, the implied volatility will be provided by your broker or option research platform in real time. I suggest using the implied volatility for a short-term at-the-money option as a proxy for the expected level of volatility in the DTRRR calculations.

All three of the explanatory variables are directly related to the expected price change of the underlying security. In other words, higher prices, longer holding periods, and greater expected volatility will all increase the expected change in price of the underlying security.

The following formula can be used to calculate the expected price change of the underlying security: RUT. The actual values used in the example were from the close on April 18, 2013.

IV = Annualized Implied Volatility
UP = Underlying Price
EPC = Expected Price Change
EXP represents the Excel function e raised to a power
e = 2.718281828

$$EPC = UP * (EXP (IV * ((HPD / 365) \wedge 0.5)) - 1)$$
$$EPC = \$901.60 * (EXP (0.2060 * ((3 / 365) \wedge 0.5)) - 1) = \$17.00$$
$$EPC = \$17.00$$

On April 18, 2013, the closing price of RUT was $901.60 and the expected level of volatility (implied volatility) was 20.60%. Based on these values, the expected price change in RUT over the subsequent three days would have been plus or minus $17.00. By using real-time values for price and implied volatility, our calculation of the expected price change, as well as the calculation of the DTRRR, will always reflect the actual market environment.

Now that we have an estimate of the expected price change in the RUT, we can combine this value with Delta and Gamma to calculate the expected price risk for the iron condor strategy, which will be the numerator (risk) in the DTRRR.

Delta is a linear estimate of the change in price for a one dollar increase in the price of the underlying security. The expected price change (EPC) is expressed as a positive number, but the realized price change could be positive or negative. Delta could also be positive or negative, but we are attempting to measure the effect of an adverse price move. In other words, we are assuming that price moves against us. As a result, when calculating the Delta Effect (DE) we first calculate the absolute value of Delta, and then multiply that value by negative one. This ensures the Delta Effect will always be negative, reflecting the expected loss from an adverse price change in the underlying security.

ABS represents the Absolute Value Excel function
Delta Effect (DE) = - ABS (Delta) * EPC
Delta Effect (DE) = - ABS ($0.25) * $17.00 = - $4.25
Delta Effect (DE) = - $4.25

Upon entry, the Delta of a market-neutral iron condor should have been very small, and it was (0.25). As a result, the Delta Effect was also relatively insignificant (- $4.25) for a $17.00 change in the price of RUT. However, Delta only captures one component of price risk. To accurately capture the total expected price risk of the iron condor, we also must include the non-linear effects of Gamma.

Gamma measures the change in Delta for a one dollar increase in the price of the underlying security, which captures the curvature of the option price function. Given that we are attempting to measure the effects of non-linearity, it should not surprise you that the Gamma Effect is an exponential function of the expected change in price. Since Gamma will always be negative for an option income strategy with positive Theta, we do not need to use the negative of the absolute value function, as we did with Delta earlier. The Gamma Effect will always be negative for option income strategies.

Gamma Effect (GE) = Gamma * (EPC ^ 2) / 2
Gamma Effect (GE) = -0.66 * ($17.00 ^ 2) / 2 = - $95.33
Gamma Effect (GE) = - $95.33

While the iron condor was constructed to be approximately Delta neutral at inception, it is impossible to eliminate Gamma risk in option income strategies. As a result, the non-linear component of the expected loss due to an adverse price change of $17.00 was significant for the iron condor on April 18, 2013 (- $95.33).

We have now calculated the Theta, Delta, and Gamma Effects for the iron condor strategy and are ready to compute the DTRRR.

DTRRR = Delta/Theta Risk/Return Ratio
DTRRR = (Delta Effect + Gamma Effect) / (Theta Effect)
DTRRR = (- $4.25 + - $95.33) / ($87.78) = - 1.13
DTRRR = - 1.13

On the entry date of the iron condor, the DTRRR was minus 1.13, which represents $1.13 of expected adverse price risk (due to Delta and Gamma) per $1.00 of expected return (due to Theta). In Chapters 7-12, we will compare and contrast the risk/return ratios for five different option income strategies, across a wide range of prices. This will provide the context to evaluate specific risk/return ratios and greatly expand your understanding of the risk and return characteristics of these strategies. For now, let's examine the variable relationships in greater detail to gain more insight into the DTRRR formula.

DTRRR versus Price

Some traders learn from studying formulas, but others prefer to see relationships portrayed visually. This section includes graphical depictions of several important variable relationships implicit in the DTRRR calculations. These graphs and the corresponding descriptions should help illustrate how price, implied volatility, Delta, Gamma, Theta, and the assumed length of the holding period affect the DTRRR.

Let's start with price. The graph in Figure 4.1 illustrates how the price of the underlying security affects the DTRRR, *holding all other variables constant – including the Greeks.* This is a very important stipulation. Normally, when we vary the price, we want to incorporate the resulting changes in the Greeks in our analysis and we will do so when we evaluate strategies in Chapters 7-12. However, for now, I want to examine one variable at a time, to ensure that you understand the mechanics of the DTRRR calculation and how changes in each variable affect the DTRRR.

Figure 4.1 is a graph of DTRRR versus the price of the underlying security. The price of the underlying security is the explanatory variable and is depicted on the x-axis (horizontal). DTRRR is the dependent variable and is shown on the y-axis (vertical). The downward sloping dotted line illustrates the relationship between the price of the underlying security and the DTRRR, holding all other variables constant.

The diamond denotes the starting value for the iron condor strategy on April 18, 2013. The other data points represent DTRRR calculations for strategies with identical Greeks and implied volatilities, but with different underlying prices. Comparable strategies with higher underlying security prices have worse (more negative) DTRRRs. Why? Higher prices with comparable implied volatilities result in greater expected price moves. Greater expected price moves increase the Delta Effect linearly and the Gamma Effect exponentially, even though we held Delta and Gamma constant. Theta was also assumed to remain constant.

At this point, we are ignoring the changes in the Greeks, because it is important to understand how and why each variable affects the DTRRR. Higher underlying security prices increase the amount of risk per unit of return, and lower underlying security prices reduce the amount of risk per unit of return, holding everything else constant.

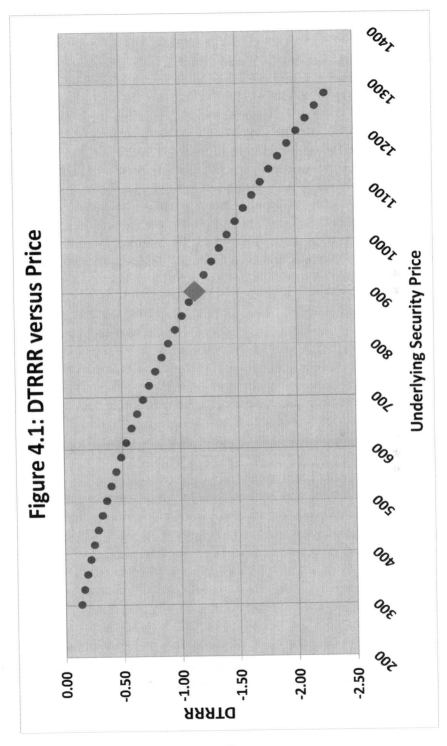

Figure 4.1: DTRRR versus Price

DTRRR versus Implied Volatility

The graph in Figure 4.2 illustrates how the annualized implied volatility (IV) affects the DTRRR, holding all other variables constant – including the Greeks. Implied volatility is derived from option prices and represents the market's estimate of the future volatility of returns for the underlying security. The IV is the explanatory variable and is depicted on the x-axis (horizontal). DTRRR is the dependent variable and is shown on the y-axis (vertical). The downward sloping dotted line illustrates the relationship between implied volatility and the DTRRR, holding all other variables constant.

The diamond denotes the starting value for the iron condor strategy on April 18, 2013. The other data points represent DTRRR calculations for strategies with identical Greek and underlying security prices, but with different annualized implied volatilities. Comparable strategies with higher IVs have worse (more negative) DTRRRs. Higher IVs with comparable underlying security prices result in greater expected price moves. Greater expected price moves increase the Delta Effect linearly and the Gamma Effect exponentially, even though we held Delta and Gamma constant.

Higher IVs increase the amount of risk per unit of return, and lower IVs reduce the amount of risk per unit of return, holding all other variables and Greek values constant.

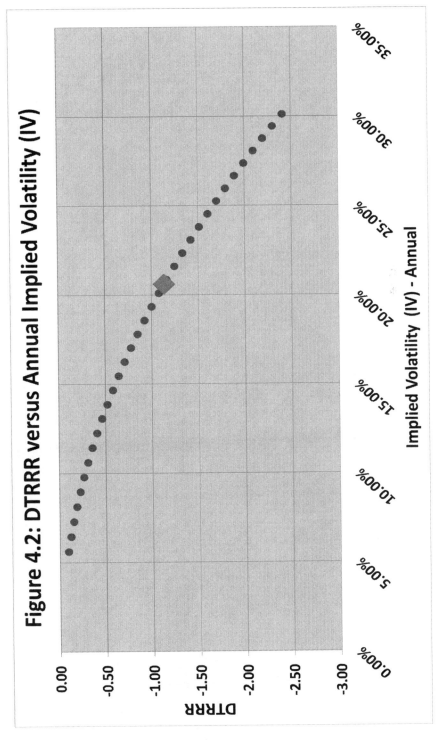

Figure 4.2: DTRRR versus Annual Implied Volatility (IV)

DTRRR versus Delta

The graph in Figure 4.3 illustrates how Delta affects the DTRRR, holding all other variables constant – including the other Greeks. Delta represents the change in the value of an option or option strategy for a one dollar increase in the price of the underlying security. Delta is the explanatory variable and is depicted on the x-axis (horizontal). DTRRR is the dependent variable and is shown on the y-axis (vertical). The peaked dotted line illustrates the relationship between Delta and the DTRRR, holding all other variables and Greeks constant.

The diamond denotes the starting value for the iron condor strategy on April 18, 2013. The other data points represent DTRRR calculations for strategies with identical underlying security prices, implied volatilities, and Greek values (except for Delta). Comparable strategies with higher magnitude values of Delta (positive or negative) have worse (more negative) DTRRRs.

Delta represents a source of price risk for an option income strategy. Since we are attempting to quantify price risk, we are interested in the effect of an adverse price move, not a favorable price move. That is the reason DTRRR reaches its peak at zero and is downward sloping as the magnitude of Delta increases, positively or negatively. Higher *absolute values* of Delta with comparable expected price changes result in greater price risk. As the magnitude of Delta increases (positively or negatively), the Delta Effect increases linearly and the Gamma Effect remains unchanged (because we assumed that Gamma remained constant).

Higher *absolute values* of Delta increase the amount of risk per unit of return, and lower *absolute values* of Delta reduce the amount of risk per unit of return, holding all other variables and Greek values constant.

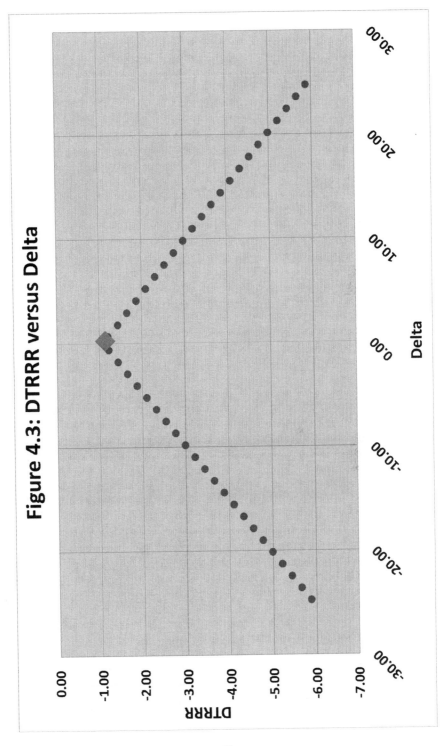

Figure 4.3: DTRRR versus Delta

DTRRR versus Gamma

The graph in Figure 4.4 illustrates how Gamma affects the DTRRR, holding all other variables constant – including the other Greeks. Gamma measures the curvature of the option price function and represents the change in Delta for a one dollar increase in the price of the underlying security. Gamma is the explanatory variable and is depicted on the x-axis (horizontal). DTRRR is the dependent variable and is shown on the y-axis (vertical). The upward-sloping dotted line illustrates the relationship between Gamma and the DTRRR, holding all other variables and Greeks constant.

The diamond denotes the starting value for the iron condor strategy on April 18, 2013. The other data points represent DTRRR calculations for strategies with identical underlying security prices, implied volatilities, and Greek values (except for Gamma). Comparable strategies with more negative values of Gamma have worse (more negative) DTRRRs.

Since Gamma will always be negative for option income strategies, which have positive Theta by definition, any price move will be an adverse price move. Therefore, negative Gamma represents a source of price risk for all option income strategies. As Gamma becomes more negative, price risk increases; specifically, the Delta Effect remains constant and the Gamma Effect increases linearly. It might be surprising that DTRRR is a linear function of Gamma, yet Gamma measures the curvature or non-linearity of the option price function. While the Gamma Effect is a non-linear effect, the non-linearity is a function of the expected change in the price of the underlying security, which we are holding constant in this example. Therefore, if Gamma becomes more negative, it will have a linear impact on the Gamma Effect and on the DTRRR.

As Gamma becomes increasingly negative, the amount of risk per unit of return increases. As the magnitude of negative Gamma decreases (Gamma becomes less negative), the amount of risk per unit of return also decreases. Again, this assumes that all other variables and Greek values remain constant.

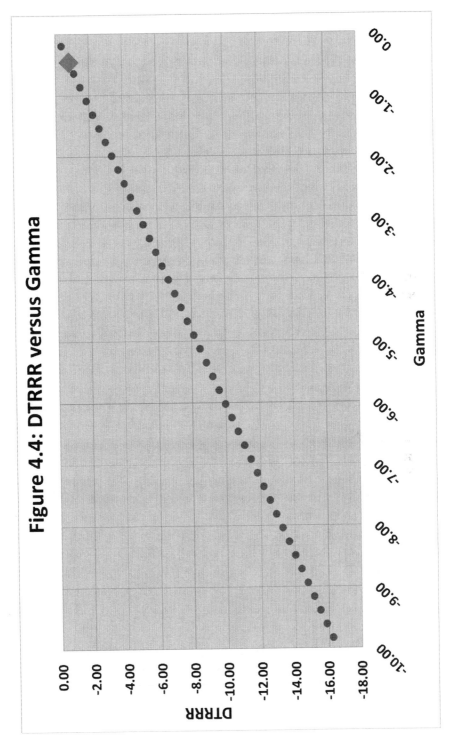

Figure 4.4: DTRRR versus Gamma

DTRRR versus Theta

The graph in Figure 4.5 illustrates how Theta affects the DTRRR, holding all other variables constant – including the other Greeks. Theta measures the daily change in the value of an option strategy due to the passage of time. Theta is the explanatory variable and is depicted on the x-axis (horizontal). DTRRR is the dependent variable and is shown on the y-axis (vertical). The upward-sloping curved dotted line illustrates the relationship between Theta and the DTRRR, holding all other variables and Greeks constant.

The diamond denotes the starting value for the iron condor strategy on April 18, 2013. The other data points represent DTRRR calculations for strategies with identical underlying security prices, implied volatilities, and Greek values (except for Theta). Theta represents the source of return or income for option income strategies, so comparable strategies with higher values of Theta have better (less negative) DTRRRs.

Theta is linear with respect to the Theta Effect (return), but increasing Theta will not have a linear effect on the DTRRR. Increases in Theta will improve the DTRRR, but at a decreasing rate. This is because Theta is in the *denominator* of the risk/return calculation. Increases in Theta will increase the denominator, but the numerator (risk) will always be negative. Therefore, increases in Theta will cause the DTRRR to approach zero, but it will never be positive.

Conversely, decreases in Theta will eventually cause Theta to approach zero. As it does so, the DTRRR will become more and more negative and the rate of change in the DTRRR will continue to increase. The rapid increase in the magnitude (increasingly negative) of the DTRRR as Theta decreases exemplifies the importance of monitoring Theta for all option income strategies.

By definition, Theta cannot be less than or equal to zero for option income strategies, or they would cease to be option income strategies. The DTRRR only applies to option income strategies with positive Theta and negative Gamma. Note, this is not a limitation of the DTRRR, because we should never own any former option income strategy that no longer has positive Theta.

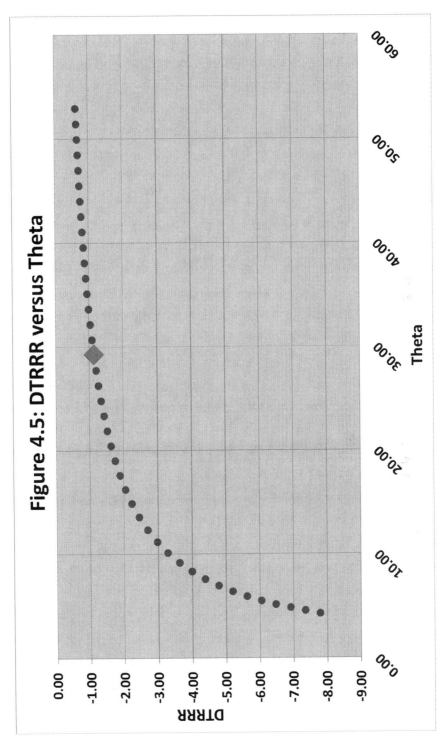

As Theta increases, the DTRRR improves; the amount of risk per unit of return decreases at a decreasing rate. As Theta decreases, the DTRRR deteriorates; the amount of risk per unit of return increases at an increasing rate – assuming all other variables and Greek values remain constant.

DTRRR versus Holding Period

Earlier in this chapter, we used an assumed number of calendar days in the holding period to calculate the Theta, Delta, and Gamma Effects. We used three days for the calculations, but postponed a discussion of the rationale behind this selection.

HPD represents the number of calendar days used in the calculation of the DTRRR. The graph in Figure 4.6 illustrates how HPD affects the DTRRR, holding all other variables constant.

HPD is the explanatory variable and is depicted on the x-axis (horizontal). DTRRR is the dependent variable and is shown on the y-axis (vertical). The upward-sloping curved dotted line illustrates the relationship between HPD and the DTRRR, holding all other variables and Greeks constant.

The diamond denotes the starting value for the iron condor strategy on April 18, 2013, based on a three-day holding period. The other data points represent DTRRR calculations for strategies with identical underlying security prices, implied volatilities, and Greek values, but with a different holding period. The DTRRR becomes less negative (improves) as the length of the holding period increases, but the rate of improvement decreases. As the holding period continues to increase, the DTRRR will eventually peak and may begin to decline.

Why does the DTRRR initially increase as the holding period increases? The reason is that the prospective return is a linear function of time, but the expected future change in price is proportional to the square root of time, not to time itself. As a result, the expected return (due to Theta) increases at a faster rate than the expected risk (due to Delta and Gamma), as the length of the holding period increases.

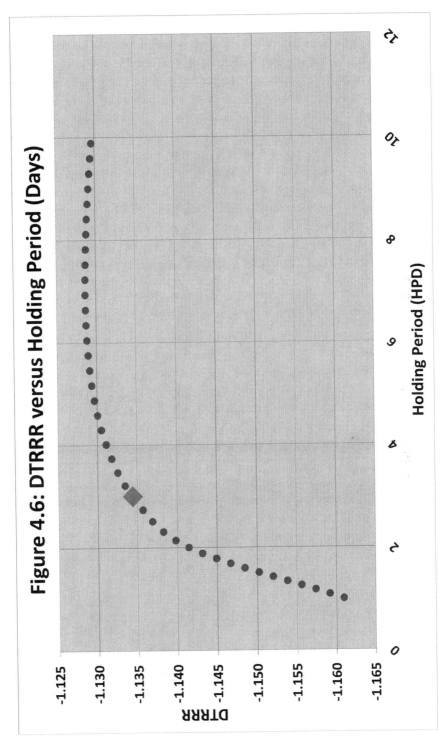

Figure 4.6: DTRRR versus Holding Period (Days)

Using an assumed holding period of one day would significantly overstate the risk relative to the return for most practical holding periods. Based on the chart in Figure 4.6, using an assumed value of three calendar days results in a more representative DTRRR calculation. Note, the HPD assumption is independent of your expected strategy holding period. You might plan to hold your iron condor strategy for 30 days, but to do so, you would need to manage and monitor your risk from day to day and from week to week. As a result, the holding period used in the DTRRR calculation should be much shorter.

I suggest using a holding period of three or four calendar days. Feel free to modify this value slightly, but I strongly suggest selecting a single HPD value for all of your risk/return calculations. This will help you manage your option income strategies objectively and consistently. It will also help you develop an intuitive understanding of how the risk/return ratios change in different market environments for different option income strategies.

Evaluation of the DTRRR

Now that we have reviewed the components of the DTRRR calculation and examined the variable relationships, we are able to evaluate the DTRRR using the framework introduced in Chapter 3. To review:

Ideally, tools used to create and manage market-neutral option income strategies would:

1. be applicable to all market-neutral option income strategies,
2. be suitable for creating "optimal" option income strategies,
3. facilitate the establishment of objective entry, exit, and adjustment rules,
4. include elements of both risk and return in the same measure or metric,
5. provide a numerical value or values that would allow meaningful comparisons across time and among different strategies, and
6. incorporate the unique characteristics of the specific market environment in the calculation of risk and return.

The DTRRR obviously includes elements of both risk and return in a single metric. It provides numerical values that are comparable across time and among all option income strategies. A DTRRR of minus 1.13 on any given day for any given strategy would be directly comparable to a DTRRR of minus 1.13 on any other day for any other strategy.

The DTRRR also incorporates the unique characteristics of the specific market environment. Unlike the simple heuristics presented in Chapter 3, the DTRRR incorporates the real-time price of the underlying security and the real-time expected level of volatility in the calculation of risk and return. As the market environment changes, the effects of these changes will automatically be included in the DTRRR.

The variables used to calculate the DTRRR apply to all option income strategies, so the resulting DTRRR is suitable for creating "optimal" option income strategies. An option income strategy with a DTRRR of minus 1.13 offers a lower (better) level of risk per unit of return than an option income strategy with a DTRRR of minus 2.50. As a result, we could use the DTRRR to identify and create option income strategies with the best (least negative) DTRRR.

Given that the DTRRR formula generates specific values that are applicable to any option income strategy, in any market environment, for any underlying security, we can use the DTRRR to establish a universal set of objective entry, exit, and adjustment rules. In other words, the DTRRR will allow us to manage all option income strategies consistently with a single risk/return framework.

5 VEGA/THETA RISK/RETURN RATIO (VTRRR)

The DTRRR introduced in Chapter 4 relates price risk to the return potential of an option income strategy, but price risk is only one component of market risk. Many traders ignore the Vega risk inherent in most option income strategies and do so at their own peril.

Vega, like Delta, is a measure of market risk, which means that we would like to minimize Vega in our market-neutral option income strategies. While Delta measures the risk of a change in the price of the underlying security, Vega measures the risk of a change in implied volatility. Specifically, Vega measures the change in the value of an option or option strategy for a 1% increase in the annual implied volatility of the expected future returns of the underlying security.

In equity markets, volatility and price move in opposite directions. When equity prices rise, implied volatility and realized volatility typically fall. When equity prices decline, implied and realized volatility usually rise. The magnitude of the change in volatility is often highly (but negatively) correlated with the magnitude of the change in equity prices. During extended bear markets and even during short-term periods of market uncertainty, implied volatility can change dramatically from day to day.

The solid line in Figure 5.1 depicts the Russell 2000 Volatility Index (RVX) from 2004 through late 2013 (left vertical axis). The RVX is an estimate of the implied volatility of 30-day options on the RUT. The solid RVX line corresponds to the values on the vertical axis on the left side of the chart.

The dashed line in Figure 5.1 represents the average daily change in the RVX Index. The dashed line represents the daily volatility of volatility. The RVX daily volatilities are expressed as percentages and they are associated with the vertical axis on the right side of the chart.

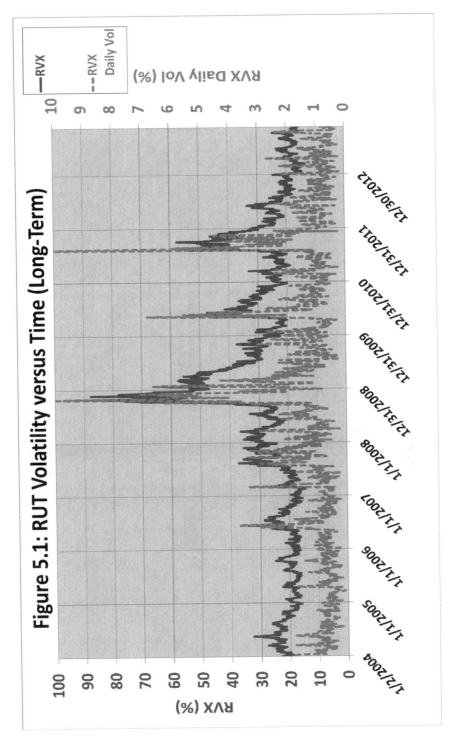

Figure 5.1: RUT Volatility versus Time (Long-Term)

During the great recession of 2008, the RVX spiked to almost 90%. When the RVX is elevated, the RVX daily volatility typically increases as well. During 2008 and again in 2011, the daily RVX volatility increased to over 10%. In other words, the average change in the annualized implied volatility of 30-day options on the RUT index was over 10% per day. This compares to a typical change of less than 1% per day. Vega can have an enormous impact on strategy returns and it is critical to incorporate the current volatility environment when estimating Vega risk.

VTRRR

The Vega/Theta Risk/Return Ratio (VTRRR) represents the expected loss (risk) incurred by an option income strategy due to an adverse change in implied volatility, divided by the expected gain (return) earned if the price of the underlying security remained constant.

By definition, the value of this ratio will always be negative for option income strategies. The passage of time will result in a gain for option income strategies – assuming all other variables (price, implied volatility, and interest rates) remain constant. Therefore, the VTRRR denominator, which represents prospective return, will always be positive.

While Vega could contribute positively to the return of an option income strategy in certain circumstances, the numerator of the VTRRR measures the risk of an *adverse* change in implied volatility (Vega Effect). As a result, the numerator will always be negative.

We would like to reduce the magnitude of risk (the numerator) and increase prospective return (the denominator); therefore, we would like the magnitude of the VTRRR to be as small a negative number as possible, which would reflect a low level of Vega risk per unit of return.

The calculations of the expected gain from the passage of time and the expected loss due to an adverse change in implied volatility are very similar to those presented in Chapter 4.

As a reminder, you will not need to do these calculations manually. I created an Excel spreadsheet that contains several macros that will do all of the required risk/return calculations. The formulas and examples are included to facilitate your application of the risk/return ratios in practice.

VTRRR Formulas & Sample Calculations

The calculation of the expected gain from the passage of time is identical to Chapter 4. Theta equals the daily change in the value of an option strategy, holding all other variables constant. As explained earlier, we will assume a calculation holding period of three calendar days. To estimate the effect of the passage of time over the assumed three calendar-day holding period, we would multiply Theta by three. The general formulas below will work for any number of days.

HPD = Number of Calendar Days in Holding Period
Theta Effect (TE) = Theta * HPD
Theta Effect (TE) = \$29.26 * 3 = \$87.78
Theta Effect (TE) = \$87.78

The prospective gain from holding the iron condor strategy over three calendar days was \$87.78, assuming all other variables remained constant. This is the same formula that we used to calculate the Theta Effect in Chapter 4 and the result is the same. This formula only approximates the actual gain due to the passage of time, but is appropriate for our purposes.

The calculation of the expected loss from an adverse change in implied volatility is very similar to the calculation of the expected loss from a change in price due to Delta (the Delta Effect). When calculating the DTRRR in Chapter 4, we included the Gamma Effect.

Vomma measures the convexity of Vega, just as Gamma measures the convexity of Delta. However, the rate of change in Vega (Vomma) is not nearly as significant as the rate of change in Delta (Gamma) and Vomma is not typically available on most option analytical platforms. As a result, the Vomma Effect will not be included in the VTRRR calculation.

Before we can calculate the risk of an *adverse* change in implied volatility (Vega Effect) on the iron condor strategy, we must first calculate the expected change in the implied volatility of RUT options, over the same three calendar-day period that we used to calculate the Theta Effect.

When we calculated the expected price change (EPC) for the

DTRRR, we were able to use the annual implied volatility to calculate the expected price change over the three calendar-day holding period. Unfortunately, to use the same methodology for calculating the expected change in implied volatility (ECIV), we would need a real-time volatility of volatility measure, which is not readily available through most broker or research platforms. As a result, we will need a procedure to estimate the ECIV directly from the recent implied volatility data.

The dashed line in Figure 5.1 was the RVX daily volatility, which represents the daily volatility of the implied volatility (DVIV) of RUT options. We will use the DVIV to calculate the expected change in implied volatility over the three calendar-day holding period (ECIV).

However, before we proceed, let's examine the method used to calculate the RVX daily volatility. The RVX daily volatility represents the root mean square daily change in implied volatility over trailing 5-day periods. This is not nearly as complicated as it sounds.

To calculate the daily volatility of implied volatility (DVIV) using the RVX Index:

1. Calculate the daily changes in RVX = Today's RVX – Yesterday's RVX
2. Square the daily changes in RVX (from step 1)
3. Calculate the 5-day average of the squared daily changes in RVX (from step 2)
4. Calculate the square root of the average of the squared daily change in RVX (from step 3)

This calculation is very similar to the formula for a population standard deviation, except the daily changes in implied volatility deviations are calculated relative to zero, not relative to the mean. These calculations are also provided in the Excel spreadsheet. The resulting RVX daily volatility represents an estimate of the expected daily change in implied volatility based on the recent volatility of implied volatility (DVIV).

Implied volatility changes rapidly in response to price movements, so it is imperative to use a recent IV data sample when calculating the DVIV as a proxy for the future daily volatility of implied volatility. We are using RUT in our examples, which is the reason for using the RVX Index in our volatility calculations.

If you were using SPX or NDX options, you would use the VIX

Index or VXN Index respectively for your volatility calculations. If you were trading an income strategy using options on an individual security that does not have a quoted volatility index, you would need to use implied volatility data derived from options on that specific underlying security. This data may be available through your broker and will be available from third-party vendors.

The DVIV is an estimate of the *daily* change in the implied volatility based on recent IV data. However, our calculation of the Vega Effect and the VTRRR will need to account for the expected change in IV over our assumed three calendar-day holding period (ECIV), rather than the expected change in IV for a single trading day (DVIV).

This calculation is complicated by the difference between calendar days and trading days. Most platforms calculate Theta using calendar days, not trading days. As a result, our calculation of the Theta Effect is based on three calendar days, not three trading days. Unfortunately, the average daily change in implied volatility (DVIV) was based on trading days. Therefore, when we calculate the expected change in IV over our three calendar-day holding period, we will need to account for the difference between trading days and calendar days.

We will use the following formula to calculate the expected change in implied volatility of RUT options (ECIV) over our assumed three calendar-day holding period. The actual values used in the example were from the entry date of an iron condor on April 18, 2013.

HPD = Number of Calendar Days in Holding Period
DVIV = Daily Volatility of Implied Volatility
ECIV = Expected Change in Implied Volatility over the Holding Period

$$\text{ECIV} = \text{DVIV} * ((\text{HPD} * (5 / 7))\,\wedge\,0.5)$$
$$\text{ECIV} = 2.57 * ((3 * (5 / 7))\,\wedge\,0.5)$$
$$\text{ECIV} = 3.76$$

In the preceding example, HPD represents the three-calendar day holding period. The average daily change in implied volatility on April 18, 2013 was 2.57, which means an average daily IV change of 2.57% over the preceding five trading days. The DVIV value of 2.57

was calculated using the four step process described earlier.

The number of calendar-days in the holding period was multiplied by (5/7) to convert trading days to calendar days. The change in IV over time is a function of the square root of time. The resulting estimate of the expected change in IV over our three calendar-day holding period was 3.76, which represents 3.76%.

Figure 5.2 is a graph of the RVX index (solid line-left vertical axis) and the RVX daily volatility (dashed line-right vertical axis) from January 1, 2013 through April 18, 2013. The daily volatility of the RVX index on April 18, 2013 was 2.57, the last value on the far right-side of the chart (diamond). As illustrated in the chart, the RVX and RVX daily volatility had recently spiked, which increased the expected change in IV (ECIV) over our assumed three calendar-day holding period. Using a relatively short five-day period allows the EVIV and ECIV to respond quickly to changing volatility environments.

Now that we have an estimate of the expected change in IV for RUT options, we can combine this value with Vega to calculate the expected Vega risk for the iron condor strategy, which will be the numerator (risk) in the VTRRR.

Vega is a linear estimate of the change in price for a 1% increase in implied volatility. The expected change in implied volatility (ECIV) is expressed as a positive number, but the realized volatility change could be positive or negative. Vega could also be positive or negative, but we are attempting to measure the effect of an adverse change in implied volatility.

In other words, we are assuming that implied volatility moves against our option income strategy. As a result, when calculating the Vega Effect (VE) we first calculate the absolute value of Vega, and then multiply that value by negative one. This ensures the Vega Effect will always be negative, reflecting the expected loss from an adverse change in implied volatility.

ABS represents the Absolute Value Excel function
Vega Effect (VE) = - ABS (Vega) * ECIV
Vega Effect (VE) = - ABS (- \$81.90) * 3.76 = - \$308.12
Vega Effect (VE) = - \$308.12

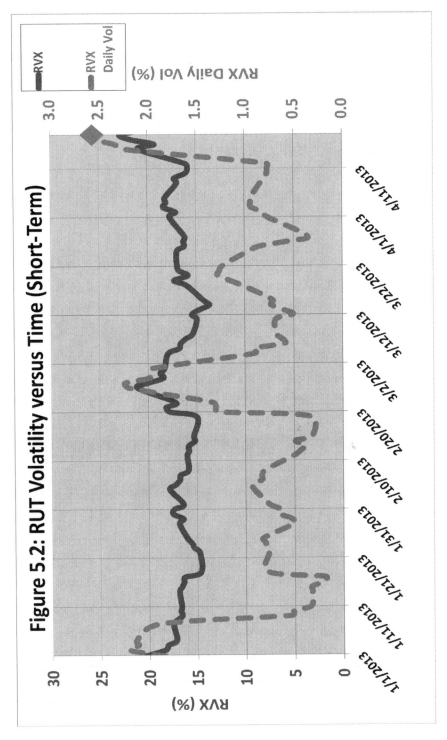

Figure 5.2: RUT Volatility versus Time (Short-Term)

You may recall from Chapter 4 that the Delta Effect was very small (-$4.25), but the Vega Effect was quite large, even on the entry date of the iron condor. By choosing the appropriate strike prices, it is possible to construct a Delta-neutral iron condor. Unfortunately, it is not possible to construct a Vega-neutral iron condor. Selling OTM options and buying options that are further out of the money in the same expiration month will always result in negative Vega. When the expected change in IV is elevated, as it was on April 19, 2013, the Vega Effect will be significant.

We have now calculated the Theta and Vega Effects for the iron condor strategy and are ready to compute the VTRRR.

VTRRR = Vega/Theta Risk/Return Ratio
VTRRR = (Vega Effect) / (Theta Effect)
VTRRR = (- $308.12) / ($87.78) = - 3.51
VTRRR = - 3.51

On the entry date of the iron condor, the DTRRR was minus 1.13, which represents $1.13 of expected adverse price risk (due to Delta and Gamma) per $1.00 of expected return (due to Theta). In contrast, the VTRRR was minus 3.51, which signifies $3.51 of expected adverse implied volatility risk (due to Vega) per $1.00 of expected return (due to Theta). The VTRRR was over three times the DTRRR, indicating over three times the level of risk per unit of return.

We will analyze a number of popular option income strategies in detail in Chapters 7-12, but it is clear that managing and monitoring Vega risk is critical to the success of option income strategies. Let's examine the variable relationships in greater detail to gain more insight into the VTRRR formula.

VTRRR versus IV Daily Volatility

This section includes graphical depictions of several important variable relationships implicit in the VTRRR calculations. These graphs and the corresponding descriptions should help illustrate how the daily volatility of IV, Vega, Theta, and the assumed length of the holding period affect the VTRRR.

Let's start with the IV daily volatility. The graph in Figure 5.3

illustrates how the daily volatility of IV affects the VTRRR, holding all other variables constant – including the Greeks. Figure 5.3 is a graph of VTRRR versus the daily volatility of IV. The IV daily volatility is the explanatory variable and is depicted on the x-axis (horizontal). VTRRR is the dependent variable and is shown on the y-axis (vertical). The downward sloping dashed line illustrates the relationship between the IV daily volatility and the VTRRR, holding all other variables constant.

The diamond denotes the starting value for the iron condor strategy on April 18, 2013. The other data points represent VTRRR calculations for strategies with identical Greeks and implied volatilities, but with different expected daily changes in implied volatility. Comparable strategies with higher expected changes in implied volatility have worse (more negative) VTRRRs. Greater expected changes in implied volatility increase the Vega Effect and the VTRRR linearly.

Higher expected changes in implied volatility increase the amount of risk per unit of return, and lower expected changes in implied volatility decrease the amount of risk per unit of return, holding everything else constant. During periods when the IV daily volatility is high, Vega exposure is particularly important to option income strategies.

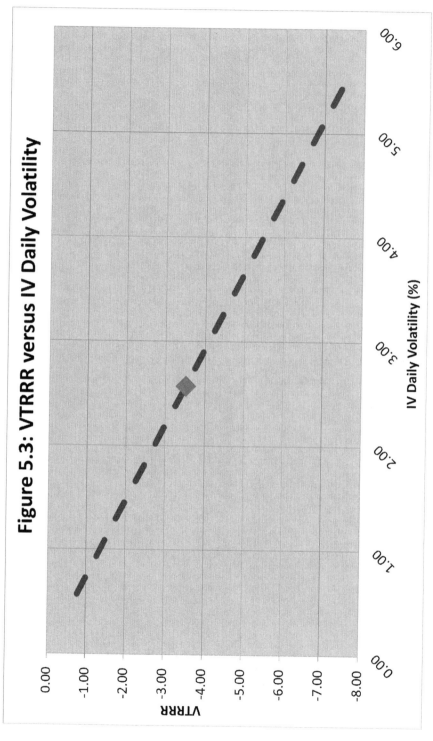

Figure 5.3: VTRRR versus IV Daily Volatility

VTRRR versus Vega

The graph in Figure 5.4 illustrates how Vega affects the VTRRR, holding all other variables constant – including the other Greeks. Vega represents the change in the value of an option or option strategy for a 1% increase in implied volatility. Vega is the explanatory variable and is depicted on the x-axis (horizontal). VTRRR is the dependent variable and is shown on the y-axis (vertical). The peaked dashed line illustrates the relationship between Vega and the VTRRR, holding all other variables and Greeks constant. You should note that the graph of VTRRR versus Vega is very similar in shape and interpretation to the graph of DTRRR versus Delta in Chapter 4 (Figure 4.3).

The diamond in Figure 5.4 denotes the starting value for the iron condor strategy on April 18, 2013. The other data points represent VTRRR calculations for strategies with identical underlying security prices, implied volatilities, and Greek values (except for Vega). Comparable strategies with higher magnitude values of Vega (positive or negative) have worse (more negative) VTRRRs.

Vega represents a source of volatility risk for an option income strategy. Since we are attempting to quantify volatility risk, we are interested in the effect of an adverse change in IV, not a favorable change in IV. That is the reason VTRRR reaches its peak at zero and is downward sloping as the magnitude of Vega increases, positively or negatively. Higher *absolute values* of Vega with comparable expected price changes result in greater volatility risk. As the magnitude of Vega increases (positively or negatively), the Vega Effect increases linearly.

Higher *absolute values* of Vega increase the amount of risk per unit of return, and lower *absolute values* of Vega reduce the amount of risk per unit of return, holding all other variables and Greek values constant.

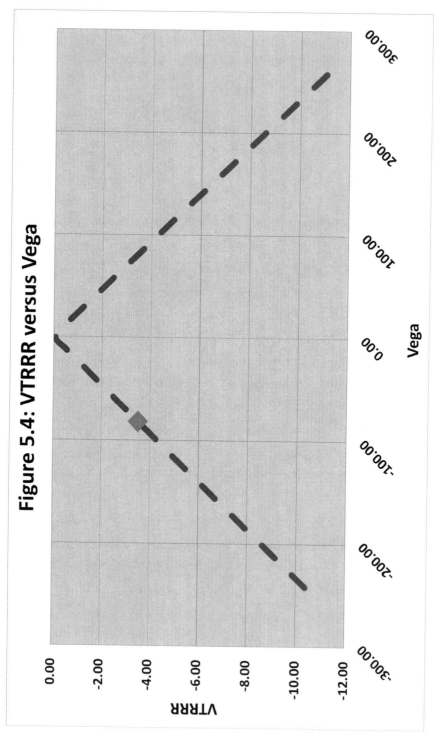

Figure 5.4: VTRRR versus Vega

VTRRR versus Theta

The graph in Figure 5.5 illustrates how Theta affects the VTRRR, holding all other variables constant – including the other Greeks. Theta measures the daily change in the value of an option strategy due to the passage of time. Theta is the explanatory variable and is depicted on the x-axis (horizontal). VTRRR is the dependent variable and is shown on the y-axis (vertical). The upward-sloping curved dashed line illustrates the relationship between Theta and the VTRRR, holding all other variables and Greeks constant. The graph of VTRRR versus Theta is very similar in shape and interpretation to the graph of DTRRR versus Theta in Chapter 4 (Figure 4.5).

The diamond in Figure 5.5 denotes the starting value for the iron condor strategy on April 18, 2013. The other data points represent VTRRR calculations for strategies with identical underlying security prices, implied volatilities, IV daily volatilities, and Greek values (except for Theta). Theta represents the source of return for option income strategies, so comparable strategies with higher values of Theta have better (less negative) VTRRRs.

Theta is linear with respect to the Theta Effect (return), but increasing Theta will not have a linear effect on the VTRRR. Increases in Theta will improve the VTRRR, but at a decreasing rate. This is because Theta is in the denominator of the risk/return calculation. Increases in Theta will increase the denominator, but the numerator (risk) will always be negative. Therefore, increases in Theta will cause the VTRRR to approach zero, but it will never be positive.

Conversely, decreases in Theta will eventually cause Theta to approach zero. As it does so, the VTRRR will become more and more negative and the rate of change in the VTRRR will continue to increase. By definition, Theta cannot be less than or equal to zero for option income strategies, or they would cease to be option income strategies. The VTRRR only applies to option income strategies with positive Theta.

As Theta increases, the VTRRR improves; the amount of risk per unit of return decreases at a decreasing rate. As Theta decreases, the VTRRR deteriorates; the amount of risk per unit of return increases at an increasing rate – assuming all other variables and Greek values remain constant.

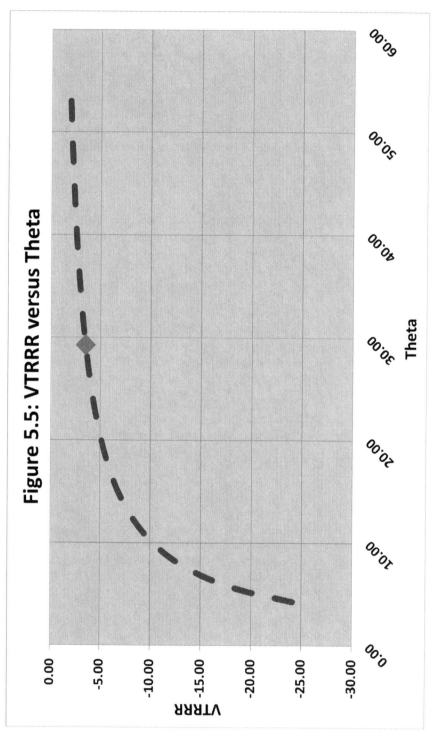

Figure 5.5: VTRRR versus Theta

VTRRR versus Holding Period

HPD represents the number of calendar days used in the calculation of the VTRRR. The graph in Figure 5.6 illustrates how HPD affects the VTRRR, holding all other variables constant.

HPD is the explanatory variable and is depicted on the x-axis (horizontal). VTRRR is the dependent variable and is shown on the y-axis (vertical). The upward-sloping curved dashed line illustrates the relationship between HPD and the VTRRR, holding all other variables and Greeks constant.

The diamond denotes the starting value for the iron condor strategy on April 18, 2013, based on a three-day holding period. The other data points represent VTRRR calculations for strategies with identical underlying security prices, implied volatilities, and Greek values, but with a different holding period. The VTRRR becomes less negative (improves) as the length of the holding period increases, but the rate of improvement decreases. As the holding period continues to increase, the VTRRR will continue to improve.

The expected return (due to Theta) increases at a faster rate than the expected risk (due to Vega), as the length of the holding period increases. As explained in Chapter 4, I suggest using a holding period of three or four calendar days, which will provide a representative value of the VTRRR.

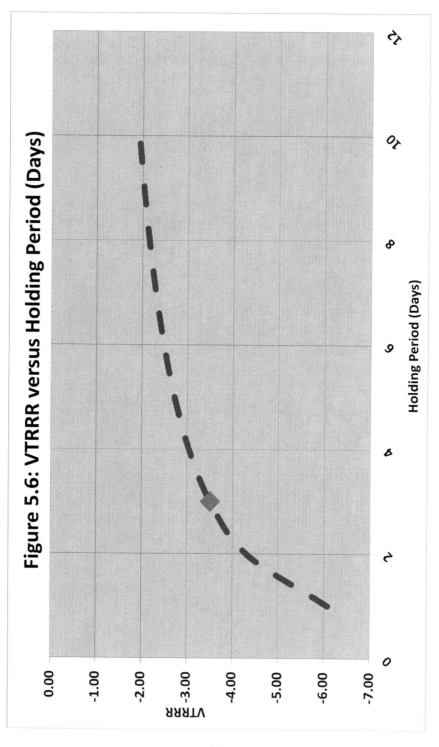

Evaluation of the VTRRR

Now that we have reviewed the components of the VTRRR calculation and examined the variable relationships, we are able to evaluate the VTRRR using the framework introduced in Chapter 3. To review:

Ideally, tools used to create and manage market-neutral option income strategies would:

1. be applicable to all market-neutral option income strategies,
2. be suitable for creating "optimal" option income strategies,
3. facilitate the establishment of objective entry, exit, and adjustment rules,
4. include elements of both risk and return in the same measure or metric,
5. provide a numerical value or values that would allow meaningful comparisons across time and among different strategies, and
6. incorporate the unique characteristics of the specific market environment in the calculation of risk and return.

The VTRRR obviously includes elements of both risk and return in a single metric. It provides numerical values that are comparable across time and among all option income strategies. A VTRRR of minus 3.51 on any given day for any given strategy would be directly comparable to a VTRRR of minus 3.51 on any other day for any other strategy.

The VTRRR also incorporates the unique characteristics of the specific market environment. Unlike the simple heuristics presented in Chapter 3, the VTRRR incorporates a timely estimate of the daily change in IV and a real-time value for Vega. As the market environment changes or the Vega of the strategy changes, the effects of these changes will automatically be included in the VTRRR.

The variables used to calculate the VTRRR apply to all option income strategies, so the resulting VTRRR is suitable for creating "optimal" option income strategies. An option income strategy with a VTRRR of minus 3.51 offers a lower (better) level of risk per unit of return than an option income strategy with a VTRRR of minus 7.52. As a result, we could use the VTRRR to identify and create option income strategies with the best (least negative) VTRRR.

Given that the VTRRR formula generates specific values that are applicable to any option income strategy, in any market environment, for any underlying security, we can use the VTRRR to establish a universal set of objective entry, exit, and adjustment rules. In other words, the VTRRR will allow us to manage all option income strategies consistently with a single risk/return framework.

Finally, the VTRRR ratio is directly comparable to the DTRRR ratio; both provide objective estimates of the expected level of risk per unit of return and both are based on the current market environment and real-time Greek values. As a result, we will not need separate objective functions or rules for VTRRR and DTRRR to create and manage our option income strategies.

6 RHO/THETA RISK/RETURN RATIO (RTRRR)

This chapter will introduce the Rho/Theta Risk/Return Ratio (RTRRR), which will complete our set of tools for constructing, evaluating, and managing option income strategies. Rho, like Delta and Vega, is a measure of market risk. While Delta measures the risk of a change in the price of the underlying security, and Vega measures the risk of a change in implied volatility, Rho measures the risk of a change in interest rates. Specifically, Rho measures the change in the value of an option or option strategy for a 1% increase in the risk-free interest rate.

Changes in interest rates affect option values through the implicit leverage (borrowing or lending) embedded in call and put options. In addition, changes in interest rates affect the expected future return distribution of the underlying security. Finally, interest rates also affect the present value of future option payoffs.

Depending on the strategy and the interest rate environment, Rho can be sizeable and interest rate risk can be significant. However, the Federal Reserve has kept short-term interest rates near zero from 2008 through the present in 2014. As a result, interest rate volatility has been virtually non-existent during that period. Given the recent low level of interest rate volatility, many traders ignore Rho when managing their option income strategies.

The solid line in Figure 6.1 depicts the 90-day T-Bill rates from 1980 through late 2013 (left vertical axis). The 90-day T-Bill rate was used as a proxy for the short-term risk-free interest used to value options. The dashed line in Figure 6.1 represents the average daily changes in the 90-day T-Bill rate (right vertical axis), or the daily interest rate volatilities, which are expressed as percentages.

During the 1980s, short-term interest rates approached 20% and the daily changes in short-term rates neared 0.50%. In other words, the average changes in the 90-day T-bill rate in the 1980s came close to 0.50% per day. Short-term interest rates are now near zero and the average daily change in the 90-day T-Bill rate has dropped to less than 0.01%. That explains why interest rate risk is frequently ignored by today's traders.

While I concede that interest rate risk is currently minimal for most option income strategies, it is important to remember that the daily interest rate volatility in 1980 was 50 times greater than it is today. And we could experience comparable levels of extreme interest rate volatility in the future.

While the values of Rho are relatively modest for most option income strategies and the level of interest rate volatility is currently at historical lows, the risk/return ratios presented in this book were designed to manage any option income strategy in any market environment.

The RTRRR formulas are very similar to those used to calculate the VTRRR. In addition, the variable relationships of the RTRRR are analogous to the VTRRR relationships. As a result, the explanations in this chapter will not be as comprehensive as those in Chapters 4 and 5. However, all formulas and graphs for the RTRRR will be provided.

RTRRR

The Rho/Theta Risk/Return Ratio (RTRRR) represents the expected loss (risk) incurred by an option income strategy due to an adverse change in interest rates, divided by the expected gain (return) earned if the price of the underlying security remained constant.

As was the case for the DTRRR and the VTRRR, the value of the RTRRR will always be negative for option income strategies. The Theta Effect in the denominator of the RTRRR will always be positive, since Theta will always be positive for all option income strategies by definition. The numerator of the RTRRR measures the risk of an *adverse* change in the risk-free interest rate (Rho Effect). As a result, the numerator will always be negative.

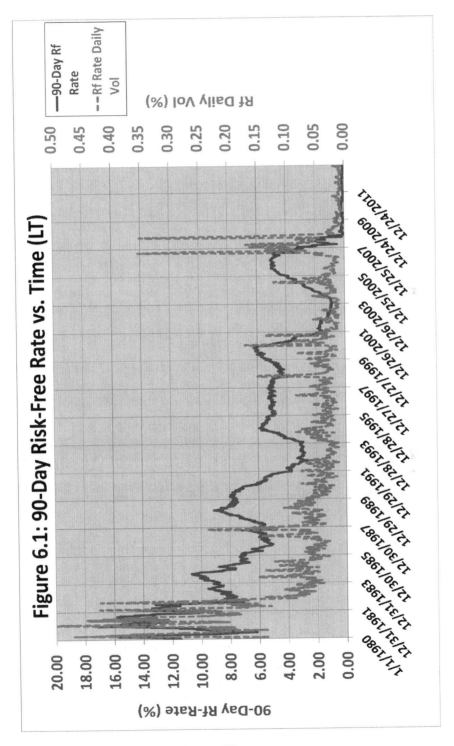

Figure 6.1: 90-Day Risk-Free Rate vs. Time (LT)

RTRRR Formulas & Sample Calculations

The calculation of the expected gain from the passage of time is identical to the computation used in Chapters 4 and 5. As explained earlier, we will assume a calculation holding period of three calendar days. To estimate the effect of the passage of time over the assumed three calendar-day holding period, we would multiply Theta by three.

HPD = Number of Calendar Days in Holding Period
Theta Effect (TE) = Theta * HPD
Theta Effect (TE) = \$29.26 * 3 = \$87.78
Theta Effect (TE) = \$87.78

The prospective gain from holding the iron condor strategy over three calendar days was \$87.78, assuming all other variables remained constant. The calculation of the expected loss from an adverse change in interest rates is comparable to the calculation of the expected loss from a change in implied volatility due to Vega (the Vega Effect).

Before we can calculate the risk of an *adverse* change in interest rates (Rho Effect) on the iron condor strategy, we must first calculate the expected change in the interest rates, over the same three calendar-day period that we used to calculate the Theta Effect. We will use the same procedure introduced in Chapter 5 to convert the recent daily historical volatility to a three-day expected change in the risk-free interest rate (ECRF).

The dashed line in Figure 6.1 was the daily volatility of the 90-day risk-free rate (DVRF). We will use the DVRF to calculate the expected change in the risk-free interest rate over the three calendar-day holding period (ECRF).

The daily volatility of the 90-day risk free interest rate represents the root mean square daily change in the risk-free rate over a trailing 22-trading-day period. Interest rates are not nearly as volatile as implied volatility, which allows us to use a longer historical period when calculating interest rate volatility.

To calculate the daily volatility of the risk-free interest rate (DVRF):

1.   Calculate the daily changes in RF Rate = Today's RF Rate – Yesterday's RF Rate

2.   Square the daily changes in the RF Rate (from step 1)

3.   Calculate the 22-day average of the squared daily changes in RF Rate (from step 2)

4.   Calculate the square root of the average of the squared daily change in RF Rate (from step3)

The DVRF is an estimate of the *daily* change in the implied volatility based on recent interest rate data. However, our calculation of the Rho Effect and the RTRRR will need to account for the expected change in the risk-free rate over our assumed three calendar-day holding period (ECRF), rather than the expected change in the risk-free rate for a single trading day (DVRF).

As was the case with the Vega Effect, when we calculate the expected change in the risk-free rate over our three calendar-day holding period, we will need to account for the difference between trading days and calendar days.

We use the following formula to calculate the expected change in the risk-free rate (ECRF) over our assumed three calendar-day holding period. The actual values used in the example were from the entry date of an iron condor on April 18, 2013.

HPD = Number of Calendar Days in Holding Period
DVRF = Daily Volatility of RF Rate
ECRF = Expected Change in RF Rate

ECRF = DVRF * ((HPD * (5 / 7)) ^ 0.5)
ECRF = 0.0095 * ((3 * (5 / 7)) ^ 0.5)
ECRF = 0.0139

The average daily change in the risk-free rate on April 18, 2013 was 0.0095%, which means an average daily interest rate change of 0.0095% over the preceding 22 trading days. The resulting estimate of the expected change in the risk-free rate over our three calendar-day holding period was 0.0139, which represents 0.0139%. This is an extremely low level interest rate volatility, which has been artificially depressed by the extremely accommodative Federal Reserve policy. The DVRF value of 0.0095 was calculated using the four-step process described earlier.

Figure 6.2 is a graph of the 90-day risk-free rate (solid line-left vertical axis) and the daily risk-free rate volatility (dashed line-right vertical axis) from January 1, 2013 through April 18, 2013. The daily volatility of the risk-free interest rate index on April 18, 2013 was 0.0095%, the last value on the far right-side of the chart (diamond).

The artificially low level of short-term interest rates and interest rate volatility is clearly evident in the chart. The average level of short-term rates was approximately 0.10% and the average daily interest rate volatility was less than 0.01%.

We can now combine the estimated change in the risk-free interest rate (ECRF) with Rho to calculate the expected Rho Effect for the iron condor strategy, which will be the numerator (risk) in the RTRRR.

Rho is a linear estimate of the change in price for a 1% increase in the risk-free interest rate. As was the case in the calculation of the Delta and Vega Effects, we will assume that interest rates always move against our option income strategy. As a result, when calculating the Rho Effect (RE), we first calculate the absolute value of Rho, and then multiply that value by negative one. This guarantees the Rho Effect will always be negative, reflecting the expected loss from an adverse change in the level of interest rates.

ABS represents the Absolute Value Excel function
Rho Effect (RE) = - ABS (Rho) * ECRF
Rho Effect (RE) = - ABS ($1.14) * 0.0139 = - $0.0159
Rho Effect (RE) = - $0.0159

You may recall from Chapter 4, that the Delta Effect was very small (-$4.25), but the Rho Effect was infinitesimal (- $0.0159). Not only was the value of Rho for the iron condor strategy extremely small, but the expected three calendar-day change in the risk-free rate was barely above 0.01%. The resulting Rho Effect was less than $0.02 on a position requiring $6,857 of required capital. However, the iron condor strategy used in this example has minimal exposure to changes in interest rates. An alternative strategy in a more volatile market environment would have resulted in much greater interest rate risk.

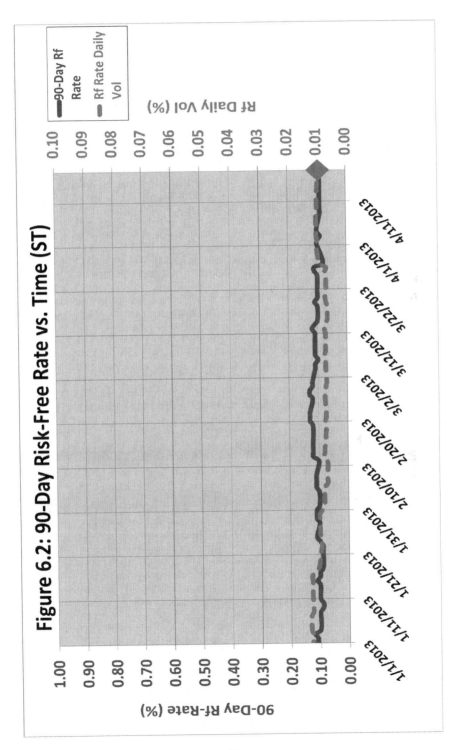

Figure 6.2: 90-Day Risk-Free Rate vs. Time (ST)

Choosing an example from the opposite extreme, the value of Rho for an ATM calendar spread with a short position in the front month option and a long position in a two-year leap would have been over $5,400 (compared to $1.14 in the earlier example). If the daily interest rate volatility would have spiked to 0.35 (as it did as recently as 2008), the resulting Rho Effect for the calendar spread would have ballooned to minus $2,765 (compared to minus $0.0159 in the preceding example). The Rho Effect can be significant for certain strategies in high volatility environments.

We have now calculated the Theta and Rho Effects for the iron condor strategy and are ready to compute the RTRRR.

RTRRR = Rho/Theta Risk/Return Ratio
RTRRR = (Rho Effect) / (Theta Effect)
RTRRR = (- $0.0159) / ($87.78) = - 0.0002
RTRRR = - 0.0002

On the entry date of the iron condor, the RTRRR was minus 0.0002, which signifies $0.0002 of expected adverse interest rate risk (due to Rho) per $1.00 of expected return (due to Theta). The level of interest rate risk for the iron condor strategy relative to the expected return was truly insignificant. However, as demonstrated earlier, the RTRRR could be significant in certain situations.

RTRRR versus Risk-Free Rate Daily Volatility

This section includes graphical depictions of several important variable relationships inherent in the RTRRR calculations. These graphs and the corresponding descriptions should help illustrate how the daily volatility of risk-free (RF) interest rates, Rho, Theta, and the assumed length of the holding period affect the RTRRR.

Let's begin with the RF-rate daily volatility. The graph in Figure 6.3 illustrates how the daily volatility of the RF-rate affects the RTRRR, holding all other variables and Greeks constant. Figure 6.3 is a graph of RTRRR versus the RF-rate daily volatility. The RF-rate daily volatility is the independent variable and is depicted on the x-axis (horizontal). RTRRR is the dependent variable and is shown on the y-axis (vertical).

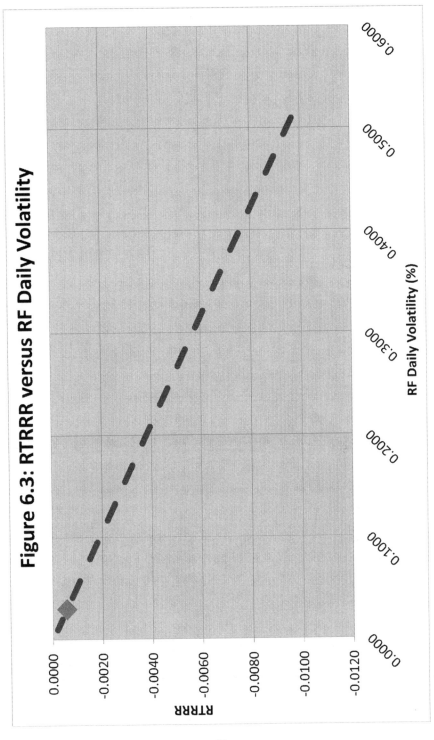

Figure 6.3: RTRRR versus RF Daily Volatility

The downward sloping dashed line illustrates the relationship between the daily volatility of the risk-free interest rate and the RTRRR, holding all other variables constant.

The diamond denotes the starting value for the iron condor strategy on April 18, 2013. The other data points represent RTRRR calculations for strategies with identical Greeks, but with different expected daily changes in the risk-free interest rate. Comparable strategies with higher expected changes in the risk-free interest rate have worse (more negative) RTRRRs. Greater expected changes in the risk-free interest rate increase the Rho Effect and the RTRRR linearly.

Higher expected changes in the risk-free interest rate increase the amount of risk per unit of return, and lower expected changes in the risk-free interest rate decrease the amount of risk per unit of return, holding everything else constant.

However, in order for the RTRRR to be a significant concern, the volatility of the risk-free interest rate must be very high *and* the magnitude of Rho for the option income strategy must also be very high. As you can see from the chart in Figure 6.3, even elevated levels of daily volatility coupled with a very low value of Rho ($1.14) would result in very low levels of interest rate risk per unit of return.

RTRRR versus Rho

The graph in Figure 6.4 illustrates how Rho affects the RTRRR, holding all other variables and Greeks constant. Rho represents the change in the value of an option or option strategy for a 1% increase in the risk-free interest rate. Rho is the explanatory variable and is depicted on the x-axis (horizontal). RTRRR is the dependent variable and is shown on the y-axis (vertical). The peaked dashed line illustrates the relationship between Rho and the RTRRR, holding all other variables and Greeks constant. You should note that the graph of RTRRR versus Rho is analogous to the graph of DTRRR versus Delta in Chapter 4 (Figure 4.3) and the graph of VTRRR versus Vega in Chapter 5 (Figure 5.4).

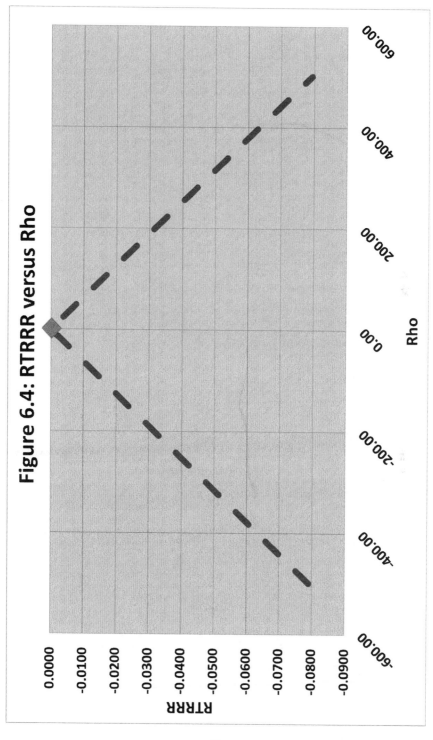

Figure 6.4: RTRRR versus Rho

The diamond in Figure 6.4 denotes the starting value for the iron condor strategy on April 18, 2013. The other data points represent RTRRR calculations for strategies with identical underlying security prices, implied volatilities, and Greek values (except for Rho). Comparable strategies with higher magnitude values of Rho (positive or negative) have worse (more negative) RTRRRs.

Since we are attempting to quantify interest rate risk, we are interested in the effect of an *adverse* change in interest rates, not a favorable change in interest rates. That is the reason RTRRR reaches its peak at zero and is downward sloping as the magnitude of Rho increases, positively or negatively. Higher *absolute values* of Rho with comparable expected price changes result in greater volatility risk. As the magnitude of Rho increases (positively or negatively), the Rho Effect increases linearly.

Higher *absolute values* of Rho increase the amount of risk per unit of return, and lower *absolute values* of Rho reduce the amount of risk per unit of return, holding all other variables and Greek values constant. The resulting values of the RTRRR in Figure 6.4 are still very low due to the artificially low level of interest rate volatility.

RTRRR versus Theta

The graph in Figure 6.5 illustrates how Theta affects the RTRRR, holding all other variables and Greeks constant. Theta measures the daily change in the value of an option strategy due to the passage of time. Theta is the explanatory variable and is depicted on the x-axis (horizontal). RTRRR is the dependent variable and is shown on the y-axis (vertical). The upward-sloping curved dashed line illustrates the relationship between Theta and the RTRRR, holding all other variables and Greeks constant. The graph of RTRRR versus Theta is analogous to the graph of VTRRR versus Theta in Chapter 5 (Figure 5.5).

The diamond in Figure 6.5 denotes the starting value for the iron condor strategy on April 18, 2013. Theta represents the source of return for option income strategies, so comparable strategies with higher values of Theta have better (less negative) RTRRRs.

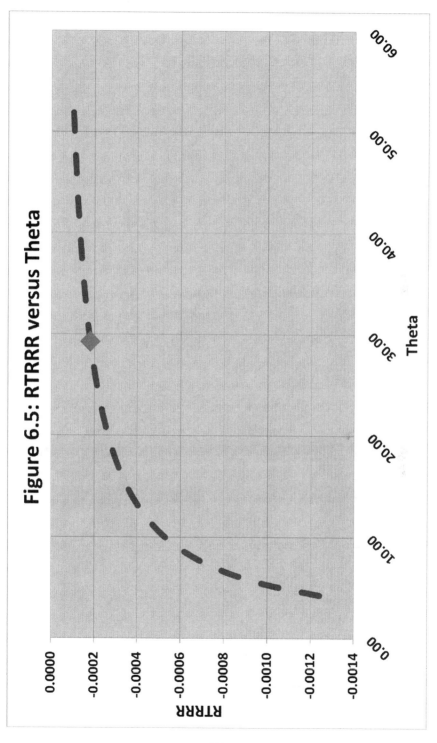

Figure 6.5: RTRRR versus Theta

Increases in Theta will improve the RTRRR, but at a decreasing rate because Theta is in the denominator of the risk/return calculation. Increases in Theta will increase the denominator, but the numerator (risk) will always be negative. Therefore, increases in Theta will cause the RTRRR to approach zero, but it will never be positive.

Conversely, decreases in Theta will eventually cause Theta to approach zero. As it does so, the RTRRR will become more and more negative and the rate of change in the RTRRR will continue to increase.

As Theta increases, the RTRRR improves; the amount of risk per unit of return decreases at a decreasing rate. As Theta decreases, the RTRRR deteriorates; the amount of risk per unit of return increases at an increasing rate – assuming all other variables and Greek values remain constant.

RTRRR versus Holding Period

HPD represents the number of calendar days used in the calculation of the RTRRR. The graph in Figure 6.6 illustrates how HPD affects the RTRRR, holding all other variables constant.

HPD is the explanatory variable and is depicted on the x-axis (horizontal). RTRRR is the dependent variable and is shown on the y-axis (vertical). The upward-sloping curved dashed line illustrates the relationship between HPD and the RTRRR, holding all other variables and Greeks constant.

The diamond denotes the starting value for the iron condor strategy on April 18, 2013, based on a three-day holding period. The RTRRR becomes less negative (improves) as the length of the holding period increases, but the rate of improvement decreases. As the holding period continues to increase, the RTRRR will continue to improve.

As explained in Chapters 4 and 5, I suggest using a holding period of three or four days for all risk/return ratios, which will provide a representative value of the RTRRR.

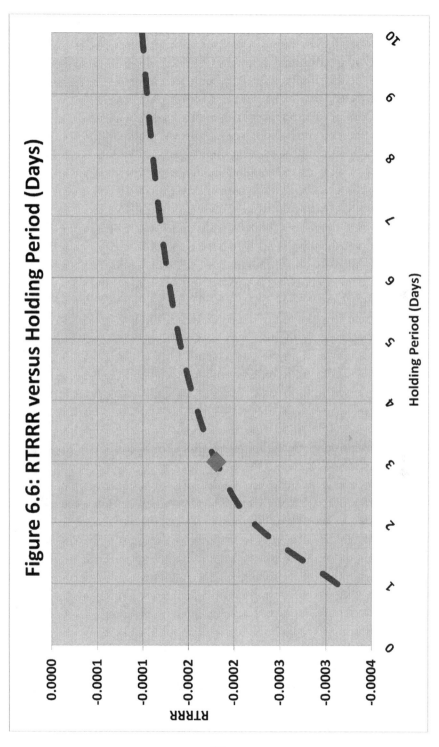

Figure 6.6: RTRRR versus Holding Period (Days)

Evaluation of the RTRRR

The RTRRR is comparable to the VTRRR and the DTRRR, which we evaluated in Chapters 4 and 5. As was the case with the DTRRR and the VTRRR, the RTRRR meets all of our criteria for creating and managing market-neutral option income strategies.

All three risk return ratios include elements of both risk and return in a single metric. They provide numerical values that are comparable across time and among all option income strategies. They also incorporate the unique characteristics of the specific market environment: price, implied volatility, IV volatility, RF volatility, etc. As the market environment changes or the strategy Greeks change, the effects of these changes will automatically be included in all three risk/return ratios.

The variables used to calculate the three risk/return ratios apply to all option income strategies, so the resulting risk/return ratios are suitable for creating "optimal" option income strategies. Given that the risk/return ratios generate specific values that are applicable to any option income strategy, in any market environment, for any underlying security, we can use them to establish a universal set of objective entry, exit, and adjustment rules.

Finally, all three ratios are directly comparable, providing objective, timely, and market-specific estimates of the expected level of risk per unit of return for any option income strategy.

7 IRON CONDORS

Now that we have thoroughly studied the DTRRR, the VTRRR, and the RTRRR, we can use these new tools to evaluate the risk and return characteristics of option income strategies in an actual market environment. In this chapter, we will analyze an iron condor established on April 18, 2013, which was the same strategy used in all sample calculations in the prior chapters. Chapters 8 - 11 will cover calendar spreads, iron butterflies, double diagonals, and hybrid combinations, respectively. In Chapter 12, we will use the risk/return ratios to compare and contrast all five of these option income strategies.

Condor Construction

There are three principal ways to construct a condor. All three require four separate option positions or legs: two long and two short. The short strikes will be positioned a significant distance above and below the current price of the underlying security. The long strikes will be located slightly beyond the short strikes, limiting the potential losses and the capital required to implement the strategy. You could construct a condor with all calls, all puts, or with a combination of call and put options.

If you used all calls or all puts to create the condor, you would be required to buy and sell options that are deeply in the money (ITM). ITM options are typically illiquid and trade infrequently. As a result, they have wider bid-ask spreads and higher transaction costs. Given that condors require four separate option positions, minimizing transaction costs is essential to the success of the condor strategy.

Iron condors require selling an OTM call credit spread and an OTM put credit spread. In other words, we would sell an OTM call option and buy a second call option further out of the money to limit our losses. We would also sell an OTM put option and buy a second put option further out of the money. The call and put spreads would both generate credits, hence the name credit spread.

Why are OTM and ATM options more liquid than ITM options? ATM and OTM put and call options are used frequently by investors as a low-cost way to hedge long and short positions, respectively. In addition, ATM and OTM options are commonly sold by option income traders. As a result, ATM and OTM options are typically more liquid than ITM options. Therefore, iron condors are more liquid and have lower transaction costs than standard condors constructed with all calls or all puts.

The easiest way to understand complex option strategies is to use strategy diagrams and the iron condor is no exception. Figure 7.1 is a partial screen capture of OptionVue's graphical analysis screen on the entry date of the iron condor on April 18, 2013. The paired values on the x-axis of the chart represent the price of RUT (the underlying security) and the percentage change of RUT from the initial value of $901.60. The left vertical axis signifies the dollar change in value of the iron condor strategy. The right vertical axis denotes the change in the value of the iron condor strategy, expressed as a percentage of the required capital.

The four lines on the chart illustrate the changes in the value of the iron condor strategy on four specific dates: T+0, T+10, T+19, and T+29. In this case, "T" stands for the trade or entry date. The values of 0, 10, 19, and 29 indicate the number of calendar days in the future. The T+0 line always represents the entry date and the solid line always denotes the expiration date of the shortest-dated option used to construct the strategy. In this case, the T+29 line represents the expiration date of the May 2013 options used to implement the iron condor strategy.

At first glance, the condor strategy diagram looks unbalanced or asymmetric, especially if you focus on the wings of the diagram. However, instead of concentrating on the wings, look at the center section of the diagram in the immediate vicinity of the initial RUT price of $901.60. Notice how flat and uniform the T+0 line is around the $901.60.

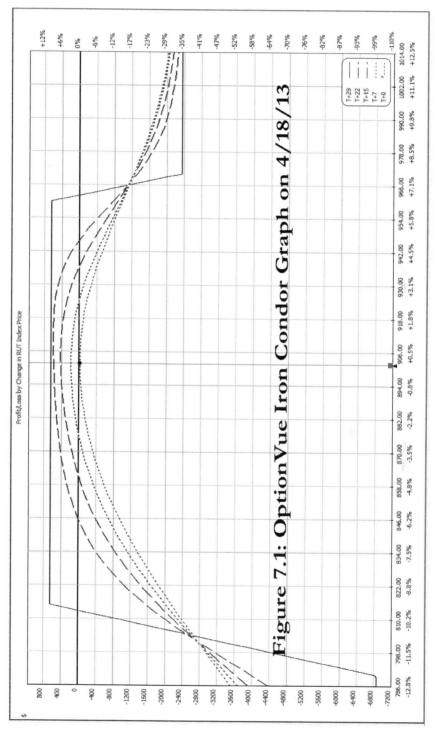

Figure 7.1: OptionVue Iron Condor Graph on 4/18/13

That is what a Delta-neutral strategy looks like and this should be your goal when you implement option income strategies. You may remember from the earlier examples that the initial Delta of the iron condor strategy was extremely small (0.25) and that is reflected by the flatness of the T+0 line.

So how do you create a Delta-neutral iron condor? Simple, the Delta of the short call should approximately offset the Delta of the short put (they should sum to zero) and the Delta of the long call should approximately offset the Delta of the long put (they should also sum to zero). If the Delta values of the put and call positions offset, then the overall strategy will be Delta-neutral.

The RUT iron condor strategy was constructed with the following four positions on April 18, 2013:

+3 RUT 970 MAY 13 Calls
- 3 RUT 960 MAY 13 Calls
- 3 RUT 815 MAY 13 Puts
+3 RUT 790 MAY 13 Puts

Figure 7.2 is a partial screen capture of OptionVue's RUT matrix on April 18, 2013. Call options are listed at the top of the image and put options are at the bottom. The strike prices are noted in the far left column. All options expire in May 2013. The market price of each option is provided in the second column (MktPr). The third column (MIV) represents the implied volatility of each option. The iron condor positions are shown in the next column (Ex.Pos). In this case, the values of plus three and minus three indicate long or short three option contracts, each with a multiplier of 100. The Delta values reported in the next column are expressed per one option contract. Finally, the time premium or time value of each option is reported in the last column (T.Prem).

According to OptionVue's interpretation of the FINRA margin requirements, the capital required to implement this iron condor strategy would have been $6,857. Note, this value was not shown in the partial screen capture image, but is calculated and provided by OptionVue.

Notice that the per-contract Delta of the long 970 calls (6.36) almost exactly offsets the Delta of the long 790 puts (-6.04) and the Delta of the short 960 calls (9.76) nearly offsets the Delta of the short 815 puts (-9.86). This explains why the iron condor was approximately Delta-neutral at inception.

Options	MAY <29> (May 17)					
	MktPr	MIV	Trade	Ex.Pos	Delta	T.Prem
990 C						
985 C	0.38	15.9%			3.29	0.38
980 C	0.48	15.7%			4.12	0.48
975 C	0.63	15.6%			5.12	0.63
970 C	0.80	15.6%		+3	6.36	0.80
965 C	1.10	15.7%			7.89	1.10
960 C	1.55	15.9%		-3	9.76	1.55
955 C	2.08	16.1%			12.0	2.08
950 C	2.73	16.3%			14.6	2.73
945 C	3.65	16.8%			17.6	3.65
940 C	4.60	16.9%			20.9	4.60
935 C	5.90	17.3%			24.6	5.90
930 C	7.30	17.5%			28.5	7.30
925 C	9.00	17.9%			32.6	9.00
920 C	11.05	18.4%			36.9	11.05
840 P	5.95	26.5%			-16.0	5.95
835 P	5.35	26.9%			-14.6	5.35
830 P	4.80	27.3%			-13.2	4.80
825 P	4.30	27.7%			-12.0	4.30
820 P	3.90	28.3%			-10.9	3.90
815 P	3.45	28.5%		-3	-9.86	3.45
810 P	3.10	29.0%			-8.94	3.10
805 P	2.78	29.4%			-8.11	2.78
800 P	2.50	29.9%			-7.35	2.50
795 P	2.25	30.3%			-6.66	2.25
790 P	2.03	30.7%		+3	-6.04	2.03
785 P	1.83	31.2%			-5.48	1.83
780 P	1.60	31.5%			-4.97	1.60
775 P	1.48	32.1%			-4.51	1.48
770 P	1.30	32.4%			-4.09	1.30

Figure 7.2: OptionVue Iron Condor Matrix on 4/18/13

Implicit Probabilities – A Digression

Delta is often used as a proxy for the probability of an option being in the money at expiration. In the case of the short 960 calls, the Delta of 9.76 implies that there was a 9.76% probability that the price of RUT would have been above 960 at expiration in May. Delta is used for this purpose in practice because it is widely available on all analytical platforms, but the resulting estimate is not precisely correct.

The Delta of a call option is derived from the value of N(d1) in the Black Scholes Option Pricing Model (BSOPM). N(d2) is the correct term from the BSOPM to use if you want to estimate the probability a call option expires in the money. N(d1) and N(d2) represent the cumulative normal density function for the BSOPM variables d1 and d2.

Using Delta as a proxy for the probability of an option expiring in the money can provide some useful intuition when selecting strikes for option income strategies, but you should be aware that Delta is not the correct value to use for this purpose.

Asymmetrical Equity Directional Volatilities

If you looked carefully at the positions in the Iron Condor matrix, you probably noticed that the spread between the call strikes (10 points) was much narrower than the spread between the put strikes (25 points). You may also have observed that the strike price of the short call position ($960) was much closer to the price of RUT ($901.60) than the strike price of the short put position ($815). The strike price of the short call was only $58.4 above the price of the RUT, but the strike price of the short put was $86.6 below the price of the RUT. The strike prices are definitely asymmetric. Why?

The reason is the directional volatilities and the resulting vertical skew. As explained in Chapter 1 and illustrated in Figure 1.7, the vertical skew exposes the market's implicit assumption that near-term price declines in RUT will be larger and more dramatic than short-term price increases. While the slope and curvature of the vertical skew both change over time, the inverse relationship between strike prices and volatility has persisted in equity index options for many years.

The market assumes that *equity* prices fall much faster than they rise and this fact is reflected in option premiums and in the resulting vertical volatility skew. As a result, for put and call options with offsetting Deltas, the OTM put options will be farther below the price of the underlying security and the spread between the put strikes will be greater.

The strike prices will always be asymmetric for a Delta-neutral iron condor. If the strike prices of an iron condor were symmetric, then the resulting strategy could not be Delta neutral and the implicit return assumptions would be inconsistent with those that have prevailed in equity options for almost 30 years. Failing to recognize and account for asymmetrical directional volatilities is one of the most common mistakes made by option traders.

Condor Entry Technique

Once we identify the trades required to implement the Delta-neutral iron condor strategy, we would need to execute all four option trades to enter the position. Some traders prefer to execute the put spread and call spreads independently, "legging into" the strategy. This is just another form of market timing – which makes no sense when implementing a non-directional option income strategy. In fact, this approach increases market risk, with no compensatory increase in expected return. If we could time the market successfully, then there would be no point in trading non-directional strategies. We would simply go long or short the underlying security instead.

Remember that the Deltas of our calls and puts offset, which was the reason our iron condor strategy was Delta-neutral. If we executed the call and put spreads independently, we would incur market risk as soon as the first credit spread order was filled. In addition, with orders for both credit spreads outstanding at the same time, if the market moved, one spread would be filled at the original limit price, but the other spread would be much more difficult to fill. Independently, the put and call credit spreads are directional strategies. They are only Delta-neutral when combined and executed simultaneously.

Iron condors should always be entered using a single limit order on the 4-leg spread. This eliminates unnecessary and undesirable market risk and will typically result in lower transaction costs. Remember, there is always someone taking the other side of our trades. If our position were Delta-neutral, then their position would also be Delta-neutral.

That means that the market-maker on the other side of our Delta-neutral spread order would not incur price risk. This would make it easier and less costly for them to fill our spread order. There would be no price risk to hedge, which would allow them greater time to work out of the position at a profit.

Option income strategy transactions should always be executed using limit orders and the limit price should be as close as possible to the mid-market price. Due to artificially wide bid-ask quoted spreads, market orders should rarely be used when trading options, especially when trading options on the principal equity indices: RUT, SPX, and NDX.

Condor Risk/Return Ratios

In Chapters 4, 5 and 6, we went through a series of detailed computations, which ultimately allowed us to calculate the DTRRR, the VTRRR, and the RTRRR on the entry date of the iron condor on April 18, 2013. This analysis was instructive, but only provided a discrete snapshot of the risk/return ratios of the iron condor strategy. We are now in a position to evaluate the risk/return characteristics of the iron condor strategy over a range of possible prices. The risk/return formulas used in the remaining chapters are identical to those introduced in the prior chapters. The only difference in the following risk/return ratios is that the input values (strategy Greeks, implied volatilities, etc.) were generated by the OptionVue option valuation and risk models. Other analytical platforms should also have the ability to generate Greek and volatility values across multiple scenarios.

Figure 7.3 is a graphical summary of the DTRRR and VTRRR for the iron condor strategy on April 18, 2013. The instantaneous change in the RUT price is the dependent variable and is depicted on the x-axis. The dotted line represents the DTRRR for a range of possible instantaneous changes in the price of RUT: from minus $40 to plus $40. The DTRRR is one of the dependent variables and is plotted on the y-axis.

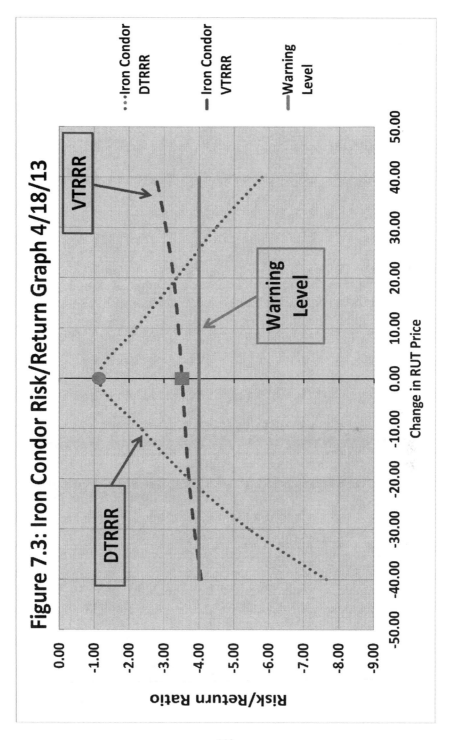

Figure 7.3: Iron Condor Risk/Return Graph 4/18/13

The dashed line illustrates the VTRRR for the same range of price changes. The VTRRR is the second dependent variable and is also plotted on the y-axis. As explained in Chapter 6, the RTRRR is currently insignificant due to the artificially low level of interest rates and interest rate volatility. As a result, the RTRRR was not included in the risk/return graph.

Finally, the solid horizontal line positioned at the constant risk/return ratio of minus 4.00 is used as an arbitrary warning level, where the risk/return characteristics of the strategy begin to become more extreme or unfavorable to the option income trader. To provide a consistent frame of reference, this warning level will be provided on the strategy graphs for all option income strategies.

Do not put too much weight on the warning level of minus 4.00. It is only provided for illustration purposes and is not a specific trading recommendation. Every trader will determine their own personal warning levels based on their unique trading style and degree of risk aversion. The trader-specific warning levels should be used to create consistent and objective adjustment points and/or exit triggers for all option income strategies.

The circle in the center of the graph represents the DTRRR on the entry date of the iron condor on April 18, 2013. We calculated this value in Chapter 4. If the price of RUT had moved up or down from the initial value of $901.60, negative Gamma would have forced the iron condor strategy to diverge from its original Delta-neutral position. The increase or decrease in the RUT price would have simultaneously caused Theta to decrease.

The result would have been an increase in price risk and a decrease in prospective return. This would have caused the DTRRR to become more negative (less attractive). If the instantaneous price change in RUT had become excessive, the DTRRR would have eventually crossed below our hypothetical warning level of minus 4.00. In this specific market environment for this particular iron condor strategy, an instantaneous price change of between $20 and $30 would have pushed the DTRRR below minus 4.00.

The square in the center of the graph represents the VTRRR on the entry date of the iron condor on April 18, 2013. We calculated this value in Chapter 5. Unlike the DTRRR, the VTRRR was relatively stable as a function of price. However, the initial value of the VTRRR (-3.51) had a much higher level of risk per unit of return than the initial value of the DTRRR (-1.13). The initial value of the VTRRR was only slightly inside the warning level of minus 4.00, even before any change in the price of RUT. A large decline in the price of RUT would have caused the VTRRR to exceed the warning level threshold of minus 4.00.

While the graphical depiction of the risk/return ratios in Figure 7.3 is easy to understand and is an efficient tool for portraying the risk and return characteristics of the iron condor over a wide range of prices, it is a blunt tool for analyzing specific values. The table in Figure 7.4 provides all of the specific values used to calculate the DTRRR and the VTRRR that were depicted in Figure 7.3.

For each RUT price level, the table provides the estimated at-the-money implied volatility, the estimated daily volatility of implied volatility, and all of the scenario-dependent Greeks for the iron condor strategy. However, OptionVue does not currently provide scenario-specific values of Rho or updated values of the daily volatility of the risk-free interest rate. As a result, these values were assumed to remain constant across all pricing scenarios. As explained earlier, the RTRRR is currently insignificant and was not included in the graphical analysis, but is included in the table.

The projected Greeks and volatility values in Figure 7.4 were used to calculate the DTRRR and VTRRR levels for each RUT pricing scenario. Scenario-specific values of DTRRR and VTRRR that violated the minus 4.00 warning threshold were shaded with white text.

Condor Optimization, Adjustments, and Exits

The preceding graph and table provide a comprehensive analysis of the risk and return characteristics of the iron condor strategy. However, it is important to note that the risk/return graph in Figure 7.3 and the scenario values in Figure 7.4 apply to a particular iron condor in a specific market environment. While it may be possible to draw some general conclusion from this analysis, the principal value of the risk/return ratios is their ability to consistently analyze any option income strategy, on any underlying security, in any market environment.

Figure 7.4: Iron Condor Risk/Return Table on 4/18/2013 (T+0)

Change In RUT Price	40.00	30.00	20.00	10.00	0.00	-10.00	-20.00	-30.00	-40.00
RUT Price	941.60	931.60	921.60	911.60	901.60	891.60	881.60	871.60	861.60
Estimated ATM IV	17.70%	18.40%	19.20%	19.90%	20.60%	21.40%	22.20%	23.10%	24.00%
IV Daily VOL	2.21	2.30	2.40	2.48	2.57	2.67	2.77	2.88	2.99
Rf Daily VOL	0.0095	0.0095	0.0095	0.0095	0.0095	0.0095	0.0095	0.0095	0.0095
Delta	-23.06	-18.63	-12.83	-6.36	0.25	6.46	12.11	17.66	23.47
Gamma	-0.36	-0.53	-0.63	-0.66	-0.66	-0.58	-0.55	-0.57	-0.58
Vega	-58.15	-72.20	-80.45	-83.15	-81.90	-78.94	-75.22	-71.14	-66.61
Theta	22.59	26.50	28.74	29.53	29.26	28.52	27.41	25.90	23.94
Rho	1.14	1.14	1.14	1.14	1.14	1.14	1.14	1.14	1.14
Warning Level	-4.00	-4.00	-4.00	-4.00	-4.00	-4.00	-4.00	-4.00	-4.00
Iron Condor DTRRR	-5.80	-4.49	-3.36	-2.22	-1.13	-2.35	-3.71	-5.44	-7.64
Iron Condor VTRRR	-2.77	-3.05	-3.27	-3.41	-3.51	-3.61	-3.71	-3.86	-4.07
Iron Condor RTRRR	-0.0002	-0.0002	-0.0002	-0.0002	-0.0002	-0.0002	-0.0002	-0.0002	-0.0002

The iron condor in this chapter was a representative example of a typical income strategy used in a monthly campaign. At entry, the iron condor had 29 calendar days remaining until expiration, and used 10-11 Delta short strikes and 6-7 Delta long strikes. There are countless possible Delta-neutral iron condors we could have constructed instead. For the short strikes, we could have used 15 Deltas, 20 Deltas, or even 25 Deltas. We could have entered the iron condor earlier, with 40 or 50 calendar days until expiration. We could have used weekly options with 7, 14, or 21 days until expiration. Which iron condor would have been the best?

In the past, it was impossible to answer that question objectively. However, using the risk/return ratios introduced in this book, it is now possible to identify the specific iron condor with the unique combination of strike prices and expiration dates that minimizes the magnitude of the DTRRR, the VTRRR, and the RTRRR in a particular market environment. In other words, we can now quantitatively identify the iron condor that delivers the lowest level of risk per unit of return.

We can't examine every possible combination of strike prices and expiration dates here, but let's briefly look at the risk/return ratios for a second prospective iron condor on the entry date of April 18, 2013. For this example, instead of using monthly options, I used weeklies. Weekly options have exploded in popularity, volume, and open interest since being introduced several years ago. As a result, transaction costs for weekly options and weekly option strategies have dropped significantly.

The specific weekly iron condor I created had eight calendar days remaining until expiration and the Deltas of the long and short strikes were comparable to those used in the monthly calendar example. Therefore, the resulting weekly iron condor was also Delta-neutral. As you would expect, the weekly iron condor had a much higher Theta, but Gamma was much worse (more negative). The magnitude of Theta and Gamma both increase as the time remaining until expiration declines. The Vega of the weekly iron condor was still negative, but the magnitude was slightly less than the Vega of the monthly iron condor.

The DTRRR of the weekly iron condor was minus 1.19, almost exactly equal to the DTRRR of the monthly iron condor (-1.13). Essentially, the increases in positive Theta and negative Gamma offset each other in the calculation of the DTRRR. However the VTRRR of the weekly iron condor (-1.09) was significantly better than the VTRRR of the monthly iron condor (-3.51).

Theta was much higher for the weekly iron condor and Vega was slightly lower. The resulting Vega risk per unit of return decreased dramatically. This simple example illustrates how we can use risk/return ratios to construct option income strategies with the lowest level of risk per unit of return.

Identifying the iron condor with the lowest level of risk per unit of return is a great starting point, but the risk/return ratios are not static. They will change as a function of changes in the market environment and they will also change as the characteristics (Greeks) of the strategy respond to changes in price, time, and volatility. As a result, we must monitor all of the risk/return ratios closely after implementing any option income strategy.

In addition to identifying the best possible iron condor on the entry date, we can also use the risk/return ratios to set objective, quantifiable, trader-specific levels where adjustments should be made to the strategy. In other words, we would adjust the strategy when the amount of risk per unit of return moved beyond our predetermined risk/return threshold.

In addition to setting specific adjustment levels, we could also use the risk/return ratios to identify the best possible trade adjustment – one that delivered the lowest level of risk per unit of return for the adjusted strategy. This is very similar to identifying the best iron condor candidate on the entry date. The only difference is that we would compare the risk/return ratios for the strategy after each prospective adjustment.

Finally, in addition to employing standard exits based on profit and loss targets, we could use specific risk/return levels to trigger objective strategy exits when the level of risk per unit of return exceeded our specific risk tolerance. We would establish these levels in advance and they would be determined by our unique level of risk aversion and by our trading philosophy.

While several strategy examples and risk/return ratio calculations are provided here and in the following chapters, the risk/return formulas outlined in this book and programmed in the supplemental spreadsheet were intended to help you use the DTRRR, the VTRRR, and the RTRRR to analyze and manage any option income strategy.

8 CALENDAR SPREADS

A *single* calendar spread requires selling an option with a near-term expiration date and buying a corresponding option of the same type (call or put), with the same strike price, but with a more distant expiration date. To construct a Delta-neutral single calendar spread, the short and long option positions must have approximately the same Deltas. This only occurs when the strike prices of the options are approximately equal to the current price of the underlying security. In other words, at-the-money (ATM) options must be used to construct Delta-neutral *single* calendar spreads.

All option income strategies have positive Theta and negative Gamma and calendar spreads are no exception. Options decay more rapidly as they approach expiration and the magnitude of Gamma increases as well. Calendar spreads generate positive Theta by selling a near-term option (that decays faster) and buying a longer-term option (that decays more slowly). Accordingly, in exchange for positive Theta, calendar traders must endure the risk of negative Gamma.

A single calendar spread with a strike price above the current price of the underlying security would have a positive Delta and would therefore be bullish. A single calendar spread with a strike price below the current price of the underlying security would have a negative Delta and would be bearish. Neither calendar spread would be Delta-neutral by itself, which is why Delta-neutral single calendars require at-the-money options.

However, it is possible to construct a Delta-neutral *double* calendar spread. Instead of using a single ATM calendar, double calendars require one bullish calendar spread with a strike price above the market price of the underlying security and one bearish calendar spread with a strike price below the market. When combined, the positive and negative Deltas of the bullish and bearish calendar

119

spreads cancel each other out, resulting in a Delta-neutral double calendar.

To enhance liquidity and reduce transaction costs, out-of-the-money options should be used to construct double calendar spreads. In other words, call calendars should be used with strike prices above the market price and put calendars should be used with strike prices below the market price.

Finally, some traders employ *triple* calendar spreads in their option income strategies. A triple calendar spread combines a single ATM Delta-neutral calendar spread with a double Delta-neutral calendar spread. By definition, if the single calendar spread and double calendar spread are both Delta-neutral, the triple calendar spread must also be Delta-neutral.

Single calendar spreads are easier and less expensive to trade, which is why they are more common than double or triple calendar spreads. As a result, a single calendar spread on the RUT was used for the calendar spread example in this chapter. Since weekly options are relatively new, monthly options were used in the calendar example with a short position in May 2013 ATM calls and a long position in June 2013 ATM calls.

When constructing single Delta-neutral calendar spreads, either ATM calls or ATM puts may be used. When deciding between calls and puts, there are two principal factors to consider: liquidity and price. Supply and demand can influence the market for ATM calls and puts. We can use volume and open interest to gage the relative liquidity of calls versus puts. Higher volume and open interest suggests greater liquidity, which should translate into lower transaction costs.

While liquidity is difficult to quantify, price is not. Implied volatility is synonymous with price. An option with high implied volatility is more expensive than an option with low implied volatility. The horizontal spread (horizontal skew) between the implied volatility of the short front-month option and the implied volatility of the long back-month option is indicative of the cost of the calendar spread.

Normally, this spread is positive. Longer-dated equity options typically have higher implied volatilities than shorter-dated equity options. However, this spread can become extreme. When the implied volatility of the back-month option exceeds that of the front-month option by more than 2% to 3%, the cost and risk of the calendar spread strategy increases significantly. We can compare the horizontal spreads of the ATM call calendar and ATM put calendar to identify the less expensive option type to use in a calendar spread.

Figure 8.1 is a partial screen capture of OptionVue's graphical analysis screen on the entry date of the calendar spread on April 18, 2013. The chart format is the same as the iron condor example in Figure 7.1. The coupled values on the x-axis of the chart represent the price and percentage price change of RUT. The left and right vertical axes illustrate the dollar and percentage changes in the value of the calendar spread, respectively.

The four lines on the chart illustrate the changes in the value of the calendar strategy for four specific dates: T+0, T+10, T+19, and T+29. The T+0 line represents the entry date and the solid line denotes the expiration date of the shortest-dated option used to construct the strategy, which in this case was May 2013.

It is important to note that T+29 is the longest practical holding period for the calendar spread strategy. While the calendar spread includes an option that expires beyond T+29, the strategy would no longer be a calendar spread after the near-term option expires. Remember, we used the short position in the near-dated option to generate positive Theta and to ensure that our calendar spread strategy was Delta-neutral. Once the near-term option expires, the calendar spread strategy would become a directional strategy with negative Theta – the exact opposite of a market-neutral option income strategy. As a result, the longest holding period for strategies that include options with multiple expiration dates will always coincide with the expiration date of the shortest-dated option used to construct the strategy.

Returning to Figure 8.1, the slope of a tangent to the T+0 line would be very flat at the initial RUT price of $901.60. This indicates that the single calendar was approximately Delta-neutral, which was our intention. This was accomplished by buying and selling ATM options with offsetting Deltas.

The RUT calendar spread strategy example was constructed with the following two positions on April 18, 2013:

- 8 RUT 905 MAY 13 Calls
+ 8 RUT 905 JUN 13 Calls

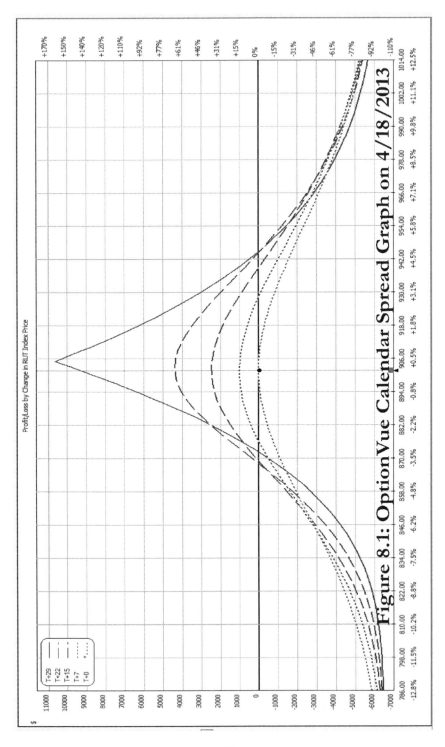

Figure 8.1: OptionVue Calendar Spread Graph on 4/18/2013

Figure 8.2 is a partial screen capture of OptionVue's RUT matrix on April 18, 2013. The format is the same as Figure 7.2 in Chapter 7, with one exception. Unlike the iron condor example, options from two different expiration months were required to construct the calendar spread. As a result, the front-month options (MAY 13) are displayed on the left, and the back-month options (JUN 13) are depicted on the right.

According to OptionVue's interpretation of the FINRA margin requirements, the capital required to implement this single calendar strategy would have been $6,531. This value was not shown in the partial screen capture image.

Notice that the per-contract Delta of the 905 MAY calls (49.5) offsets the Delta of the 905 JUN calls (49.5). The Delta values reported in the matrix are for long option positions. To determine the strategy Delta for the calendar spread, the number of contracts for each position (positive or negative) must be multiplied by their respective per contract Deltas, and then added together. Since the Delta values are the same for the ATM MAY and JUN calls and the long and short position sizes match, the strategy Delta was approximately zero, except for a slight rounding of the Delta values in the matrix.

Calendar Entry Technique

Our goal in entering all option income strategies is to minimize market risk and reduce transaction costs. As a result, single calendar spreads should be entered using one spread transaction, simultaneously selling the front-month option and buying the back-month option for a specified limit price. The spread is Delta-neutral, which also reduces the risk for the market-maker who takes the opposite side of our entry transaction. All competitive broker platforms support option spread orders and some even offer reduced commissions for spread orders. The end result of using a 2-leg spread order to enter single calendar spreads is reduced market risk and lower transactions costs.

Actuals	RUT Index		Legend			Figure 8.2: OptionVue
	901.60	-5.10	Last	Chg	Trade	Calendar Spread 4/18/13
	898.40	909.80	Low	High	Ex.Pos	

Options	MAY <29> (May 17)						JUN <64> (Jun 21)					
940 C	MktPr	MIV	Trade	Ex.Pos	Delta	T.Prem	MktPr	MIV	Trade	Ex.Pos	Delta	T.Prem
935 C	5.90	17.3%			23.7	5.90	12.70	17.0%			31.9	12.70
930 C	7.30	17.6%			27.7	7.30	14.60	17.3%			34.8	14.60
925 C	9.00	17.9%			31.9	9.00	16.60	17.5%			37.8	16.60
920 C	11.05	18.4%			36.2	11.05	18.80	17.8%			40.7	18.80
915 C	13.15	18.7%			40.6	13.15	21.15	18.0%			43.7	21.15
910 C	15.55	19.1%			45.1	15.55	23.65	18.3%			46.6	23.65
905 C >	18.15	19.5%		-8	49.5	18.15	26.30	18.5%		+8	49.5	26.30
900 C >	20.90	19.8%			53.8	19.30	29.10	18.8%			52.4	27.50
895 C	23.90	20.3%			57.9	17.30	31.95	19.0%			55.2	25.35
890 C	27.15	20.7%			61.8	15.55	35.40	19.5%			57.9	23.80
885 C	30.55	21.1%			65.6	13.95	38.55	19.8%			60.6	21.95
880 C	34.05	21.5%			69.0	12.45	41.60	19.8%			63.2	20.00
875 C	37.60	21.8%			72.2	11.00	45.10	20.1%			65.6	18.50
870 C	41.40	22.2%			75.2	9.80	48.50	20.3%			68.0	16.90
940 P	44.70	19.3%			-77.2	6.30	52.65	19.3%			-68.0	14.25
935 P	40.90	19.3%			-73.7	7.50	49.35	19.4%			-65.4	15.95
930 P	37.40	19.6%			-70.1	9.00	46.65	19.9%			-62.7	18.25
925 P	34.15	19.9%			-66.4	10.75	43.40	19.9%			-60.1	20.00
920 P	31.00	20.1%			-62.5	12.60	40.50	20.0%			-57.4	22.10
915 P	28.25	20.5%			-58.6	14.85	37.85	20.3%			-54.8	24.45
910 P	25.60	20.8%			-64.7	17.20	35.55	20.6%			-52.1	27.15
905 P >	23.30	21.2%			-60.9	19.90	33.15	20.9%			-49.5	29.75
900 P >	21.05	21.5%			-47.1	21.05	30.90	21.1%			-47.0	30.90
895 P	18.95	21.9%			-43.5	18.95	28.90	21.4%			-44.5	28.90

Double calendar spreads can also be entered as a spread trade and all four legs should be entered using a single spread transaction. Remember, the bullish and bearish calendar spreads are not market neutral. If you attempted to execute the bullish and bearish spreads using separate limit orders, you would incur market risk if one spread were executed before the other. Broker platforms and option exchanges support the vast majority of four-leg option orders.

Triple calendar spreads require six-legs, which are not currently supported by the spread book used by option exchanges. As a result, to enter a triple calendar spread, you would need to split the trades into two Delta-neutral spread orders: one limit order for the ATM single calendar spread and a second limit order for the double calendar spread. Even if one order were filled before the other, both orders would be Delta-neutral, so you would not incur any interim price risk.

Calendar Risk/Return Ratios

Figure 8.3 is a graphical summary of the DTRRR and VTRRR for the calendar spread strategy on April 18, 2013. This chart is directly comparable to the iron condor strategy chart in Figure 7.3. The DTRRR is represented by the dotted line and the VTRRR is depicted by the dashed line. Instantaneous price changes of minus $40 to plus $40 are shown in the chart. The same hypothetical warning level of minus 4.00 is used for illustration purposes.

The circle in the center of the graph represents the DTRRR on the entry date of the calendar spread on April 18, 2013. At entry, the initial DTRRR value of minus 1.15 was well inside the warning level. At this point, the price risk of the single calendar spread was consistent with the prospective return. The price risk of the calendar spread would also have been well behaved for increases in the price of RUT. The DTRRR would have remained inside the warning level for instantaneous RUT price increases of up to $30 (approximately 3.3%). Even for a $40 price increase, the DTRRR would only have moved slightly outside the warning level of minus 4.00.

The story was different for the downside. Despite being Delta-neutral at entry, the DTRRR would have deteriorated much more rapidly for a bearish move in the price of RUT. A modest $17 decline in the price of RUT would have caused the DTRRR to penetrate the warning threshold. A $40 decline in the price of RUT would have dramatically increased the price risk per unit of return; the DTRRR would have ballooned to minus 13.3.

The VTRRR graph reveals a very serious flaw in using calendar spreads to generate income. The square in the center of the graph represents the VTRRR on the entry date of the single calendar spread on April 18, 2013. Even on the entry date, the VTRRR of minus 5.04 was already well beyond the warning level. The VTRRR would have remained outside the warning level for the entire range of prospective price changes: from minus $40 to plus $40. For a price change of minus $40 in RUT, the VTRRR would have plummeted to minus 17.45, which was over four times the magnitude of the warning threshold.

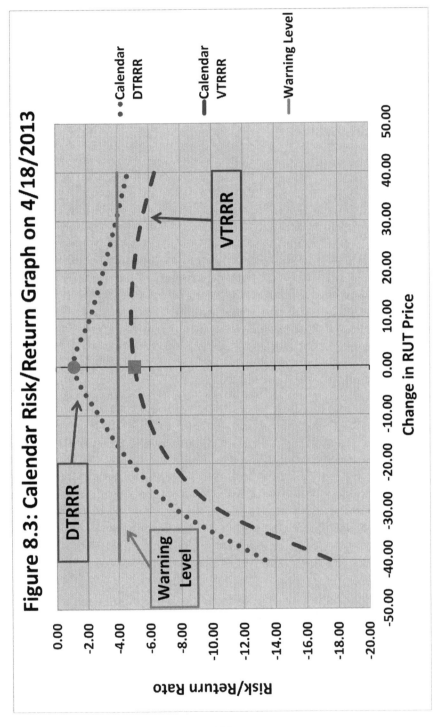

Figure 8.3: Calendar Risk/Return Graph on 4/18/2013

Clearly the amount of Vega risk per unit of return is excessive for the single calendar spread used in this example. While generalizing from a single example is not usually advisable, the amount of Vega risk per unit of return can be problematic for calendar spreads in many market environments. The table in Figure 8.4 provides all of the specific values used to calculate the DTRRR and the VTRRR that were depicted in Figure 8.3. The specific values will help us understand the source of excessive Vega risk in calendar spreads.

The format of the table in Figure 8.4 is the same as the table format used in Figure 7.4. For each RUT price level, the table provides the estimated at-the-money implied volatility, the estimated daily volatility of implied volatility, and all of the scenario-dependent Greeks for the calendar spread strategy. Scenario-specific values of DTRRR and VTRRR that violated the minus 4.00 warning threshold were shaded with white text. As you can see in Figure 8.4, the entire VTRRR row is highlighted.

If we examine the specific values in the table, we see that Vega is positive and very large at all RUT price levels. As illustrated in Figure 2.6, Vega is an increasing function of the square root of time remaining until expiration. Since calendar spreads require selling a near-term option and buying an option with a more distant expiration date, all calendar spreads have positive Vega.

The second component of the Vega Effect (VE) is the IV daily volatility, which represents an estimate of the expected daily change in implied volatility. You may recall from Figure 5.2 that the implied volatility and the IV daily volatility had spiked just prior to the date of our analysis: April 18, 2013. As a result, the estimated daily change in implied volatility on the entry date (2.57%) was elevated, which increased the magnitude of the Vega Effect even further.

Theta was not the problem, at least on the entry date. The original Theta of the calendar spread was $98.10, which was much higher than the Theta of the iron condor from Chapter 7. For prospective increases in price, Theta would have declined and Vega would have increased, which is the reason that the VTRRR would have deteriorated. It is interesting to note that the IV daily volatility would have declined had prices increased. The initial value of the IV daily volatility was 2.57%. The forecasted value of the IV daily volatility for a $40 increase in the price of RUT would have been lower: 2.21%.

Figure 8.4: Call Calendar Spread Risk/Return Table on 4/18/2013 (T+0)

(T+0) Chang In RUT Price	-40.00	-30.00	-20.00	-10.00	0.00	10.00	20.00	30.00	40.00
RUT Price	861.60	871.60	881.60	891.60	901.60	911.60	921.60	931.60	941.60
Estimated ATM IV	24.00%	23.10%	22.20%	21.40%	20.60%	19.90%	19.20%	18.40%	17.70%
IV Daily VOL	2.99	2.88	2.77	2.67	2.57	2.48	2.40	2.30	2.21
Rf Daily VOL	0.0095	0.0095	0.0095	0.0095	0.0095	0.0095	0.0095	0.0095	0.0095
Delta	70.17	59.84	43.51	22.62	-0.21	-22.15	-40.85	-54.84	-62.89
Gamma	-0.70	-1.36	-1.91	-2.25	-2.31	-2.09	-1.66	-1.12	-0.50
Vega	435.70	426.00	411.70	399.50	394.30	397.70	407.40	419.30	427.70
Theta	36.47	56.43	74.99	89.62	98.10	99.57	94.64	84.80	72.34
Rho	325.70	325.70	325.70	325.70	325.70	325.70	325.70	325.70	325.70
Warning Level	-4.00	-4.00	-4.00	-4.00	-4.00	-4.00	-4.00	-4.00	-4.00
Calendar DTRRR	-13.30	-7.89	-4.83	-2.75	-1.15	-2.19	-3.09	-3.92	-4.68
Calendar VTRRR	-17.45	-10.62	-7.42	-5.81	-5.04	-4.84	-5.03	-5.54	-6.37
Calendar RTRRR	-0.0414	-0.0268	-0.0201	-0.0168	-0.0154	-0.0152	-0.0160	-0.0178	-0.0209

This illustrates a very important relationship that affects all equity option traders. Volatility declines when equity prices increase and volatility increases when equity prices decline. In addition, the volatility of volatility is directly correlated with volatility itself. In other words, when implied volatility rises, the expected daily change in implied volatility also rises. Conversely, when implied volatility falls, the expected daily change in implied volatility also falls. The average correlation between implied volatility and the IV daily volatility was plus 0.76 historically, compared to a possible range of minus 1.0 to plus 1.0.

For prospective decreases in price, Theta would have dropped sharply and Vega would have increased. To make matters worse for the calendar spread, the IV daily volatility would have increased significantly. The Vega Effect would have increased due to the increases in Vega and in the IV daily volatility. The declines in Theta and in the Theta Effect would have compounded the problem. This is why the VTRRR would have plunged had RUT prices declined sharply.

Calendar Optimization, Adjustments, and Exits

The amount of Vega risk per unit of return was excessive for the monthly calendar spread used in this example. In fact, while the calendar spread was Delta-neutral on the entry date, it was not market-neutral. It was considerably exposed to a decline in implied volatility and was not sufficiently compensated through positive Theta to incur that amount of risk.

Many calendar traders have experienced this problem firsthand through repeated losses during low volatility environments. Every option income strategy has negative Gamma, so we would prefer a low level of realized volatility to mitigate the adverse effects of negative Gamma. Unfortunately, low levels of realized volatility often lead to declines in implied volatility, which can be devastating to monthly calendar spreads due to their unfavorable VTRRR.

We briefly examined a weekly iron condor in Chapter 7 and discovered that it significantly reduced the VTRRR relative to the monthly iron condor. Perhaps a weekly calendar spread will prove equally useful. The specific weekly calendar spread tested had eight calendar days remaining until expiration for the short call and 15 calendar days remaining for the long call. Both weekly call options had ATM strike prices of $900. The resulting weekly calendar spread was approximately Delta-neutral and the required capital was $6,342.

As was the case with the weekly iron condor, the weekly calendar spread had a much higher Theta relative to the monthly calendar, but Gamma was much worse (more negative). The Vega of the weekly calendar spread was still quite large (+ $314.3) and did not decrease as much as we might have expected relative to the monthly calendar. Remember that Vega is a function of the square root of time remaining until expiration. As a result, Vega does not decrease linearly as time-to-expiration decreases.

The DTRRR of the resulting weekly calendar spread was minus 0.73, which was slightly better than the DTRRR of the monthly calendar (-1.15). The increases in positive Theta and negative Gamma tend to offset each other in the calculation of the DTRRR. However, as was the case for the iron condor, the VTRRR of the weekly calendar spread (-1.14) was dramatically better than the VTRRR of the monthly calendar spread (-5.04).

Theta was much higher for the weekly calendar spread and Vega was slightly lower. The resulting Vega risk per unit of return decreased dramatically. Obviously we would need to examine the DTRRR and VTRRR of weekly calendar spreads over a range of prospective price changes before employing a weekly calendar spread strategy, but the impressive reduction in the magnitude of the VTRRR for the weekly calendar spread is encouraging.

We have used the risk/return ratios to expose and quantify a major flaw in monthly calendar spreads and potentially uncover a solution. A more comprehensive risk/return ratio analysis of single, double, and triple calendars over a variety of possible expiration dates could help us determine the optimal calendar spread candidate in different market environments.

In addition to identifying the best possible calendar spread candidate on the entry date, we could also use the risk/return ratios to set objective, quantifiable, trader-specific adjustment and exit levels that could be used to consistently manage all of our other option income strategies.

9 IRON BUTTERFLIES

Iron butterflies are very similar to iron condors; both strategies require the sale of a bull put credit spread and a bear call credit spread. However, there is one significant difference between iron butterflies and iron condors. When constructing the credit spreads for iron butterflies, we sell at-the-money call and put options instead of out-of-the-money call and put options. Due to the sale of at-the-money options, the values of the credit spreads are higher for iron butterflies than for iron condors. Unfortunately, the maximum payout at expiration also increases due to the wider spreads between the strike prices of the butterflies' long and short positions.

Butterflies could also be created with all calls or all puts, but that would require buying options that were significantly in the money. As explained during the introduction of iron condors in Chapter 7, in-the-money options are less liquid and typically have wider bid-ask spreads. As a result, we will use an iron butterfly example in this chapter. Monthly options were used to be consistent with the strategies examined in earlier chapters.

Figure 9.1 is a partial screen capture of OptionVue's graphical analysis screen on the entry date of the iron butterfly: April 18, 2013. The chart format is the same as the profit and loss graph formats used in prior chapters. The coupled values on the x-axis of the chart represent the price and percentage price change of RUT. The left and right vertical axes illustrate the dollar and percentage changes in the value of the iron butterfly, respectively.

The four lines on the chart illustrate the changes in the value of the iron butterfly strategy for four specific dates: T+0, T+10, T+19, and T+29. The T+0 line represents the entry date and the solid line denotes the expiration date of the shortest-dated option used to construct the strategy, which in this instance was May 2013.

131

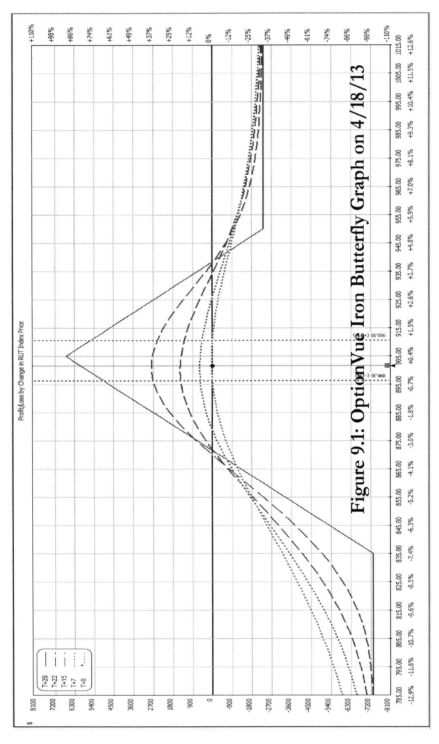

ProfitLoss by Change in RUT Index Price

Figure 9.1: OptionVue Iron Butterfly Graph on 4/18/13

As was the case with the iron condor, the iron butterfly strategy diagram appears to be unbalanced or asymmetric at the wings. However, notice how flat and uniform the T+0 line was at $901.60, which was the price of RUT on the entry date. The slope of a line tangent to the T+0 line at the price of $901.60 would be roughly zero. The slope of that tangent line is equivalent to Delta: the estimated change in the price of an option or the value of an option strategy for a one dollar increase in the price of the underlying security.

The resulting iron butterfly strategy was approximately Delta-neutral at inception, which should be our goal when implementing market-neutral option income strategies. The initial value of Delta for the iron butterfly strategy was $2.52, which was inconsequential relative to the capital required to implement the iron butterfly strategy on April 18, 2013: $7,332.

Despite being Delta-neutral at inception, the iron butterfly used in this chapter does have an asymmetric profit and loss function *at expiration*. Technically, this type of iron butterfly is called a broken-wing iron butterfly. The broken-wing designation refers to the lopsided look of the expiration profit and loss function. Due to their asymmetry, broken-wing butterflies are often used to implement directional bets, but the broken-wing iron butterfly used in this chapter was Delta-neutral, which is why it was used as an option income strategy.

Broken-wing butterflies vary the distance between the long and short strike prices, the size of the positions in the wings, or both. However, even for broken-wing butterflies, the number of long option contracts will always equal the number of short option contracts.

We construct a Delta-neutral iron butterfly the same way we construct a Delta-neutral iron condor. The Delta of the short call should approximately offset the Delta of the short put (they should sum to zero) and the Delta of the long call should approximately offset the Delta of the long put (they should also sum to zero). If the Delta values of the put and call positions offset, then the overall strategy will be Delta-neutral.

The RUT iron butterfly strategy was constructed with the following four positions on April 18, 2013:

- 2 RUT 905 MAY 13 Calls   +2 RUT 950 MAY 13 Calls

- 2 RUT 905 MAY 13 Puts   +2 RUT 835 MAY 13 Puts

Figure 9.2 is a partial screen capture of OptionVue's RUT matrix on April 18, 2013. The format is the same as the matrix layout from Figure 7.2 in Chapter 7. Notice that the per-contract Delta of the long 950 calls (13.7) almost exactly offsets the Delta of the long 835 puts (-13.5) and the Delta of the short 905 calls (49.5) nearly offsets the Delta of the short 905 puts (-50.9). This explains why the iron butterfly was approximately Delta-neutral at inception.

Options	MktPr	MIV	Trade	Ex.Pos	Delta	T.Prem
960 C						
955 C	2.08	16.2%			11.0	2.08
950 C	2.73	16.4%		+2	13.7	2.73
945 C	3.65	16.7%			16.8	3.65
940 C	4.60	16.9%			20.2	4.60
935 C	5.90	17.3%			23.9	5.90
930 C	7.30	17.6%			27.8	7.30
925 C	9.00	17.9%			32.0	9.00
920 C	11.05	18.3%			36.3	11.05
915 C	13.15	18.7%			40.7	13.15
910 C	15.55	19.1%			45.1	15.55
905 C	18.15	19.5%		-2	49.5	18.15
900 C >	20.90	19.8%			53.8	19.30
905 P	23.30	21.2%		-2	-50.9	19.90
900 P >	21.05	21.5%			-47.1	21.05
895 P	18.95	21.9%			-43.5	18.95
890 P	17.15	22.3%			-40.0	17.15
885 P	15.50	22.8%			-36.7	15.50
880 P	13.95	23.1%			-33.5	13.95
875 P	12.60	23.6%			-30.5	12.60
870 P	11.35	24.0%			-27.7	11.35
865 P	10.20	24.5%			-25.1	10.20
860 P	9.15	24.8%			-22.7	9.15
855 P	8.25	25.3%			-20.5	8.25
850 P	7.45	25.8%			-18.5	7.45
845 P	6.65	26.1%			-16.7	6.65
840 P	5.95	26.5%			-15.0	5.95
835 P	5.35	27.0%		+2	-13.5	5.35
830 P	4.80	27.3%			-12.2	4.80

Figure 9.2: OptionVue Iron Butterfly Matrix on April 18, 2013

Asymmetrical Equity Directional Volatilities

As was the case with the iron condor in Chapter 7, the spread between the call strikes (45 points) was much narrower than the spread between the put strikes (70 points). The reason for the spread difference is the asymmetrical directional volatilities in *equity* options and the resulting vertical implied volatility skew.

Equity prices fall much faster than they rise and that behavior is reflected in option premiums and in the resulting vertical volatility skew. Therefore, for put and call options with comparable Deltas, the strike prices of OTM put options will be farther below the price of the underlying security and the spread between the short and long put strikes will be greater.

The strike prices of call and put options will always be asymmetric for Delta-neutral iron butterflies and iron condors constructed with equivalent Deltas. If the strike prices were symmetric, then the resulting iron butterfly strategy would not be Delta neutral.

Iron Butterfly Entry Technique

Iron butterflies should always be entered using a single limit order on the 4-leg spread. This eliminates unnecessary and undesirable market risk and will typically result in lower transaction costs. The only way to eliminate price-related market risk is to execute all four legs simultaneously using a single spread order.

Neither of the two credit spreads would be Delta-neutral when executed separately; they would only be Delta-neutral when executed as a single unit. Delta-neutral transactions also lower the risk incurred by the market-maker taking the other side of our iron butterfly trade. The reduced risk should help lower any risk premium embedded in the bid-ask spread.

Iron Butterfly Risk/Return Ratios

Figure 9.3 is a graphical summary of the DTRRR and VTRRR for the iron butterfly strategy on April 18, 2013. This chart is analogous to the iron condor strategy chart in Figure 7.3. The DTRRR is represented by the dotted line and the VTRRR is depicted by the dashed line. Instantaneous price changes of minus $40 to plus $40 are shown in the chart. The same hypothetical warning level of minus 4.00 is used for comparison purposes.

The circle in the center of the graph represents the DTRRR on the entry date of the iron butterfly on April 18, 2013. At entry, the initial DTRRR value of minus 1.60 was worse than the iron condor, but was still well inside the warning level. The DTRRR of the iron butterfly would also have been relatively benign for increases in the price of RUT. The DTRRR would have remained inside the warning level for instantaneous RUT price increases of up to $30 (approximately 3.3%).

The price risk relative to the prospective return would have deteriorated much more rapidly had RUT prices declined. A minimal $11 decline in the price of RUT would have caused the DTRRR to penetrate the warning threshold. A $40 decline in the price of RUT would have had a shocking effect on the price risk per unit of return; the DTRRR would have exploded to minus 50.44. Note, this value was not shown on the chart. The minimum risk/return value on the y-axis in Figure 9.3 was capped at minus 20 to make it easier to interpret the remaining chart values.

At this point, it is important to recognize that the profit and loss diagram in Figure 9.1 and the risk/return graph in Figure 9.3 are similar, but there are important differences. Both charts reflect the risk and return characteristics of the iron butterfly strategy over a range of RUT prices. Figure 9.1 shows the expected profit or loss of the iron butterfly strategy. While the expected loss for the iron butterfly was worse to the downside than to the upside, the downside performance does not appear to be nearly as extreme as the asymmetry depicted in the risk/return graph in Figure 9.3. Why the apparent discrepancy?

The explanation for the seeming inconsistency is that risk/return ratios are forward-looking and profit and loss estimates are backward-looking. The profit and loss values reflect the performance of the strategy for a given price move. In contrast, the risk/return ratios measure the expected level of risk per unit of return *after* that price change has occurred.

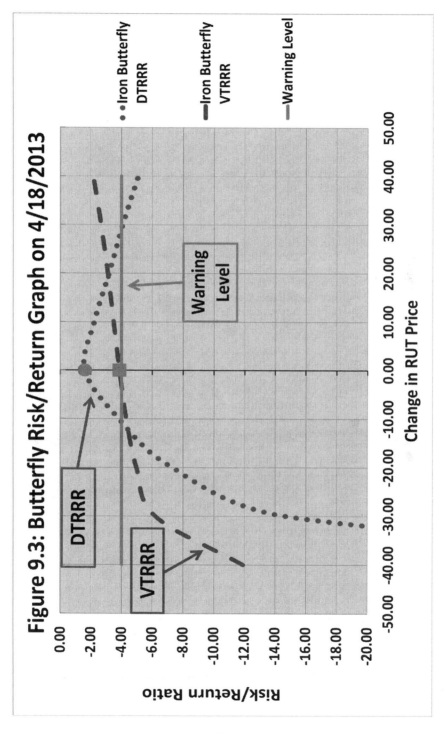

Figure 9.3: Butterfly Risk/Return Graph on 4/18/2013

The DTRRR of minus 50.44 mentioned earlier was calculated *after* an assumed price change of minus $40 in the RUT. That was the starting point for the forward-looking DTRRR calculation. The DTRRR value of minus 50.44 estimates the expected price risk per unit of return for an adverse price move that begins at minus $40 and moves even further. That is why risk/return ratios deteriorate faster than the performance of the actual option income strategy. This is exactly the behavior we want in a risk management tool. We want to be able to recognize increased risk before it adversely affects return.

The square in the center of the graph represents the VTRRR on the entry date of the iron butterfly on April 18, 2013. Even on the entry date, the VTRRR of minus 3.86 was barely inside the warning level. The VTRRR would have improved if the price of RUT had increased. For price changes of zero to plus $40, the VTRRR would have remained above the warning level.

However, if the price of RUT had declined, the VTRRR would have quickly penetrated the warning level and would have dropped to minus 11.9 after a price change of minus $40 in RUT.

The table in Figure 9.4 provides all of the specific values used to calculate the DTRRR and the VTRRR that were depicted in Figure 9.3. The format of the table in Figure 9.4 is the same as the risk/return table format used in prior chapters. For each RUT price level, the table provides the estimated at-the-money implied volatility, the estimated daily volatility of implied volatility, and all of the scenario-dependent Greeks for the iron butterfly strategy. Scenario-specific values of DTRRR and VTRRR that violated the minus 4.00 warning threshold were shaded with white text.

Large decreases in price can be perilous for the Delta-neutral iron butterfly. The DTRRR and the VTRRR deteriorate very quickly. Why does the DTRRR drop off so rapidly after price declines in RUT? The initial value of Theta was $56.96 and the iron butterfly was approximately Delta-neutral ($2.52). Gamma was minus 1.60, reflecting the cost of positive Theta. For declines in the price of RUT, Theta would have dropped sharply, all the way down to $8.80, after a $40 decline in RUT.

Figure 9.4: Iron Butterfly Risk/Return Table on 4/18/2013 (T+0)

(T+0) Chang In RUT Price	-40.00	-30.00	-20.00	-10.00	0.00	10.00	20.00	30.00	40.00
RUT Price	861.60	871.60	881.60	891.60	901.60	911.60	921.60	931.60	941.60
Estimated ATM IV	24.00%	23.10%	22.20%	21.40%	20.60%	19.90%	19.20%	18.40%	17.70%
IV Daily VOL	2.99	2.88	2.77	2.67	2.57	2.48	2.40	2.30	2.21
Rf Daily VOL	0.0095	0.0095	0.0095	0.0095	0.0095	0.0095	0.0095	0.0095	0.0095
Delta	61.83	50.65	35.85	19.09	2.52	-11.90	-22.62	-28.96	-31.03
Gamma	-0.89	-1.33	-1.63	-1.71	-1.60	-1.29	-0.86	-0.41	-0.01
Vega	-71.70	-116.10	-152.20	-172.20	-175.30	-161.00	-133.10	-97.80	-61.90
Theta	8.80	26.33	41.30	52.00	56.96	56.03	50.19	41.15	30.94
Rho	8.51	8.51	8.51	8.51	8.51	8.51	8.51	8.51	8.51
Warning Level	-4.00	-4.00	-4.00	-4.00	-4.00	-4.00	-4.00	-4.00	-4.00
Iron Butterfly DTRRR	-50.44	-14.69	-7.30	-3.81	-1.60	-2.23	-3.18	-4.08	-5.10
Iron Butterfly VTRRR	-11.90	-6.20	-4.98	-4.31	-3.86	-3.48	-3.10	-2.66	-2.16
Iron Butterfly RTRRR	-0.0045	-0.0015	-0.0010	-0.0008	-0.0007	-0.0007	-0.0008	-0.0010	-0.0013

Gamma actually would have improved, but Delta would have exploded to $61.83. In addition, the corresponding increase in volatility would have amplified the magnitude of the expected adverse price change in RUT. The magnified expected change in price, coupled with the large Delta exposure and modest Gamma risk, and very little positive Theta, would have all contributed to the very poor DTRRR.

The initial value of Vega was minus $175.30. A price decline in RUT would have reduced the magnitude of Vega, but the increase in volatility and the sharp decline in Theta would have swamped the decline in Vega. As a result, the VTRRR would have worsened quickly if RUT prices had declined.

Iron Butterfly Optimization

The amount of Vega risk per unit of return was higher than we would have liked on the entry date of the iron butterfly and both the DTRRR and VTRRR would have quickly moved beyond the warning threshold had RUT prices declined. We briefly examined alternative weekly strategies in Chapters 7 and 8 and discovered that both weekly strategies significantly reduced the VTRRRs relative to those of their respective monthly strategies.

I constructed a weekly iron butterfly on April 18, 2013 to further our examination of weekly risk/return ratios. The specific weekly iron butterfly tested had eight calendar days remaining until expiration. I selected strike prices with option Deltas that were as close as possible to the Deltas used in the monthly iron butterfly example. The resulting weekly iron butterfly was approximately Delta-neutral and the required capital was $6,497.

As we would expect, the weekly iron butterfly had a much higher Theta relative to the monthly iron butterfly, but Gamma was much worse (more negative). The Vega of the weekly iron butterfly spread was minus $135.60, which represented a notable improvement relative to the Vega of the monthly iron butterfly (- $175.30).

The DTRRR of the resulting weekly iron butterfly was minus 1.52, which was slightly better than the DTRRR of the monthly iron butterfly (-1.60). The increases in positive Theta and negative Gamma tend to offset each other in the calculation of the DTRRR. However, as was the case for the iron condor and calendar spread, the VTRRR of the weekly iron butterfly (-0.97) was dramatically better than the VTRRR of the monthly iron butterfly (-3.86).

Theta was much higher for the weekly iron butterfly and Vega was slightly lower. The resulting Vega risk per unit of return decreased dramatically. This example continues to reinforce how the risk/return ratios could be used to identify the optimal option income strategy in any market environment.

10 DOUBLE DIAGONALS

A credit spread requires the sale of a call or put option and the purchase of a second call or put option with the same expiration date, but with a strike price that is further out of the money. A diagonal spread also requires the simultaneous purchase and sale of two options of the same type (call or put), but with different expiration dates.

In Chapters 7 and 9, a put credit spread and a call credit spread were combined to create a Delta-neutral iron condor and a Delta-neutral iron butterfly, respectively. In this chapter, a diagonal call spread and a diagonal put spread will be combined to construct a Delta-neutral double diagonal spread. Options with one and two months remaining until expiration will be used to be consistent with the strategy examples in previous chapters.

There are many ways to construct a double diagonal spread and many strike prices and expiration dates from which to choose. To facilitate comparison with the iron butterfly strategy from Chapter 9, the strike prices used to create the double diagonal spread were as close as possible to those used to implement the iron butterfly. This required the sale of at-the-money (ATM) call and put options in the front-month (May 2013) and the purchase of out-of-the-money (OTM) call and put options in the back-month (June 2013). The strike prices were rounded up or down $5 as needed to ensure the double diagonal strategy was Delta-neutral at inception.

Even with purchasing OTM options in the back-month that were more expensive than the OTM options in the front-month, the put and call diagonal spreads were both created for net credits. The double diagonal strategy is interesting in that it uses two different tactics to create positive Theta. The first is that it sells ATM options and purchases OTM options. ATM options have more time premium and greater daily time decay than OTM options, which generates positive Theta for the spread. In addition, instead of buying OTM options in the front month, the double diagonal strategy purchases OTM options in the back month. Longer-term options decay more slowly than shorter-term options, which further enhances the positive Theta for the double diagonal.

The techniques used to deliver positive Theta are enlightening, but the real innovation in the double diagonal spread is its method for reducing Vega risk. ATM options have greater exposure to Vega than OTM options. As a result, when we sell ATM options and buy OTM options, the resulting strategy will have negative Vega. We observed this phenomenon with iron butterflies in Chapter 9 and to a lesser extent with iron condors in Chapter 7. Conversely, longer-dated options have greater Vega exposure than shorter-dated options, which explains why calendar spreads have positive Vega.

Do you see the opportunity to reduce risk? Iron butterflies (and iron condors) have negative Vega and calendar spreads have positive Vega. What if we integrated the general structure of the iron butterfly with the time spread component of the calendar spread? We could hedge our Vega exposure and preserve the advantages of positive Theta. That is exactly what the double diagonal spread accomplishes.

Figure 10.1 is a partial screen capture of OptionVue's graphical analysis screen on the entry date of the double diagonal spread on April 18, 2013. The chart layout is the same as the profit and loss graph formats used in prior chapters. While the double diagonal spread has elements of the iron butterfly and the calendar, its profit and loss diagram is most reminiscent of the calendar spread diagram.

The double diagonal was Delta-neutral at inception, which is consistent with the zero slope of the tangent to the T+0 line at the initial RUT price of $901.60. The initial value of Delta for the double diagonal spread strategy was $0.24 and the FINRA capital requirement (as calculated by OptionVue) would have been $9,333 on April 18, 2013. The projected performance of the double diagonal spread was relatively symmetric. The attractive profits in the center section of the chart indicate the double diagonal strategy would perform well if realized volatility were low. This trait is common to all Delta-neutral option income strategies.

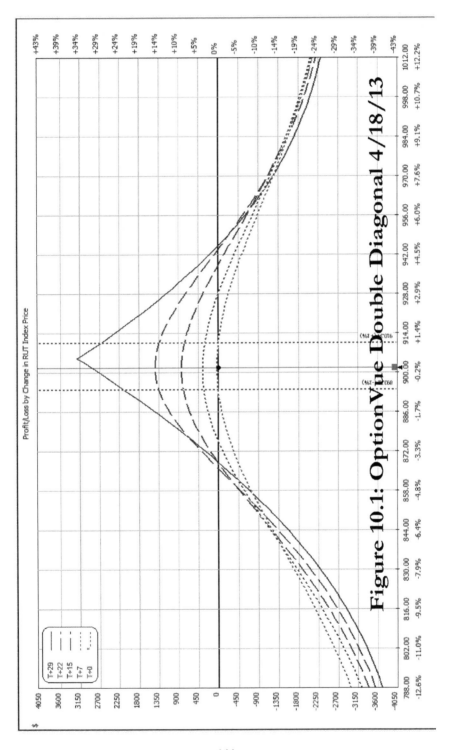

Figure 10.1: OptionVue Double Diagonal 4/18/13

We construct a Delta-neutral double diagonal spread using the same process that we used to construct the Delta-neutral iron butterfly in Chapter 9. The Delta of the short ATM call should approximately offset the Delta of the short ATM put (they should sum to zero) and the Delta of the long OTM call should approximately offset the Delta of the long OTM put (they should also sum to zero).

The RUT double diagonal strategy was constructed with the following four positions on April 18, 2013:

+1 RUT 955 JUN 13 Calls
- 1 RUT 905 MAY 13 Calls
- 1 RUT 905 MAY 13 Puts
+1 RUT 840 JUN 13 Puts

The double diagonal used the same short option positions as the iron butterfly from Chapter 9 (identical expiration dates and strike prices). The strike prices of the long OTM call and put options used to create the double diagonal were slightly different from the strikes used to construct the iron butterfly. As mentioned earlier, the JUN strike prices were rounded up or down $5 as needed to ensure the double diagonal strategy was Delta-neutral at inception.

Figure 10.2 is a partial screen capture of OptionVue's RUT matrix on April 18, 2013. The format is similar to the OptionVue RUT matrix layout from previous chapters. Notice that the per-contract Delta of the long 955 JUN calls (21.2) almost exactly offsets the Delta of the long 840 JUN puts (-22.3) and the Delta of the short 905 MAY calls (49.5) nearly offsets the Delta of the short 905 MAY puts (-50.9). The Delta values in the OptionVue matrix assume a long position of one option contract, representing 100 shares (or in this case, a multiplier of 100). The offsetting Deltas of the put and call positions guarantees the double diagonal strategy will be Delta-neutral at inception.

Options	MAY <29> (May 17)						JUN <64> (Jun 21)					
970 C	MktPr	MIV	Trade	Ex.Pos	Delta	T.Prem	MktPr	MIV	Trade	Ex.Pos	Delta	T.Prem
965 C	1.10	15.6%			6.75	1.10	4.75	15.7%			16.5	4.75
960 C	1.55	15.9%			8.66	1.55	5.70	15.9%			18.8	5.70
955 C	2.08	16.1%			11.0	2.08	6.85	16.1%		+1	21.2	6.85
950 C	2.73	16.3%			13.6	2.73	8.05	16.3%			23.7	8.05
945 C	3.65	16.7%			16.6	3.65	9.45	16.5%			26.4	9.45
940 C	4.60	16.9%			20.0	4.60	11.00	16.7%			29.1	11.00
935 C	5.90	17.3%			23.7	5.90	12.70	17.0%			31.9	12.70
930 C	7.30	17.6%			27.7	7.30	14.60	17.2%			34.8	14.60
925 C	9.00	17.9%			31.9	9.00	16.60	17.5%			37.7	16.60
920 C	11.05	18.4%			36.2	11.05	18.80	17.7%			40.6	18.80
915 C	13.15	18.7%			40.6	13.15	21.15	18.0%			43.6	21.15
910 C	15.55	19.1%			45.1	15.55	23.65	18.3%			46.5	23.65
905 C	18.15	19.5%		-1	49.5	18.15	26.30	18.5%			49.4	26.30
900 C >	20.90	19.8%			53.7	19.30	29.10	18.8%			52.3	27.50
905 P	23.30	21.2%		-1	-50.9	19.90	33.15	20.9%			-49.5	29.75
900 P >	21.05	21.5%			-47.2	21.05	30.90	21.1%			-47.0	30.90
895 P	18.95	21.9%			-43.5	18.95	28.90	21.5%			-44.5	28.90
890 P	17.15	22.3%			-40.0	17.15	26.85	21.6%			-42.1	26.85
885 P	15.50	22.8%			-36.7	15.50	25.05	22.0%			-39.7	25.05
880 P	13.95	23.1%			-33.5	13.95	23.30	22.2%			-37.4	23.30
875 P	12.60	23.6%			-30.5	12.60	21.60	22.4%			-35.2	21.60
870 P	11.35	24.0%			-27.7	11.35	20.10	22.7%			-33.1	20.10
865 P	10.20	24.5%			-25.1	10.20	18.70	23.0%			-31.1	18.70
860 P	9.15	24.9%			-22.7	9.15	17.35	23.3%			-29.1	17.35
855 P	8.25	25.3%			-20.5	8.25	16.20	23.7%			-27.3	16.20
850 P	7.45	25.8%			-18.5	7.45	15.00	23.9%			-25.5	15.00
845 P	6.65	26.1%			-16.7	6.65	13.90	24.2%			-23.9	13.90
840 P	5.95	26.5%			-15.0	5.95	12.90	24.5%		+1	-22.3	12.90

Figure 10.2: OptionVue Double Diagonal Matrix on 4/18/13

Asymmetrical Equity Directional Volatilities

As explained earlier, *equity* prices fall much faster than they rise and that behavior is reflected in option premiums and in the resulting vertical volatility skew. Therefore, for put and call options with comparable Deltas, the strike prices of OTM put options will be farther below the price of the underlying security and the spread between the short and long put strikes will be greater.

This effect is not limited to equity options in the front-month. As a result, the spread between the call strikes for the double diagonal (50 points) was narrower than the spread between the put strikes (65 points), just as we noted for the iron butterfly in Chapter 9.

Double Diagonal Entry Technique

From an execution perspective, double diagonal spreads are no different from iron butterflies or iron condors. Double diagonal spreads should always be entered using a single limit order on the 4-leg spread. As was the case for our other 4-leg option income strategies, simultaneous execution eliminates unnecessary and undesirable market risk and will typically result in lower transaction costs.

Remember, the only way to eliminate price-related market risk is to execute all four legs simultaneously using a single spread order. Neither of the two diagonal spreads would be Delta-neutral when executed separately; they would only be Delta-neutral when executed as a single unit.

Double Diagonal Risk/Return Ratios

Figure 10.3 is a graphical summary of the DTRRR and VTRRR for the double diagonal strategy on April 18, 2013. This chart is comparable to the risk/return ratio strategy charts from prior chapters. The DTRRR is depicted by the dotted line and the VTRRR is represented by the dashed line. Instantaneous price changes of minus $40 to plus $40 are provided in the chart. The hypothetical warning level of minus 4.00 is the horizontal solid line.

The circle in the center of the graph represents the DTRRR on the entry date of the double diagonal on April 18, 2013. At entry, the initial DTRRR value of minus 1.17 was better than the iron butterfly and similar to the calendar spread. For increases in the price of RUT, the DTRRR of the double diagonal would have been very similar to the DTRRRs of the iron condor, calendar spread, and the iron butterfly. The DTRRR for all of the strategies, including the double diagonal, would have remained inside or very near the warning level of minus 4.0 for instantaneous RUT price increases of up to $30 (approximately 3.3%).

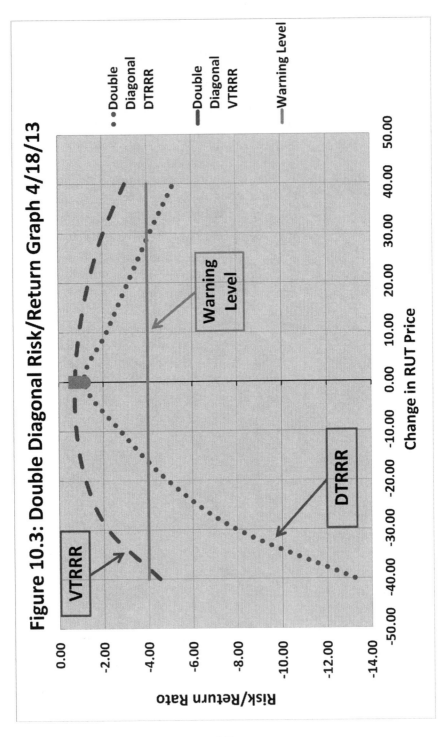

Figure 10.3: Double Diagonal Risk/Return Graph 4/18/13

As was the case with all of the strategies from the earlier chapters, the price risk relative to the prospective return would have deteriorated much more rapidly for the double diagonal had RUT prices declined. The downside DTRRR levels for the double diagonal were comparable to those of the calendar spread and better than those of the iron butterfly. A $14 decline in the price of RUT would have caused the DTRRR of the double diagonal to penetrate the warning threshold. A $40 decline in the price of RUT would have caused the DTRRR of the double diagonal to grow to minus 13.23. This was comparable to the DTRRR of the calendar spread (-13.30) and far better than the DTRRR of the iron butterfly (-50.44).

It is encouraging that the spectrum of DTRRR values for the double diagonal was no worse than that of the calendar spread and far better than the gamut of DTRRR values for the iron butterfly. However, the real benefit of the double diagonal strategy is evidenced by its distribution of VTRRR values. The square in the center of the graph represents the VTRRR on the entry date of the double diagonal on April 18, 2013. On the entry date, the VTRRR of the double diagonal was an impressive minus 0.74, which was only a fraction of the VTRRR of the calendar (-5.04) and the iron butterfly (-3.86).

By integrating option income strategies with negative and positive Vega, the double diagonal spread was able to drastically reduce exposure to Vega, without sacrificing positive Theta. On the entry date of the diagonal spread, the resulting Vega risk per unit of expected return was lower than all of the preceding strategies. While the initial value of VTRRR is promising, it is even more encouraging that the VTRRR would have remained inside the warning threshold for almost the entire range of prospective price changes.

Let's use the table in Figure 10.4 to more closely examine the risk and return characteristics of the double diagonal spread. The format of the table is the same as the risk/return table layouts used in prior chapters. The price risk per unit of prospective return is comparable to several of the earlier strategies, so let's refocus our attention on the VTRRR of the double diagonal spread.

Figure 10.4: Double Diagonal Spread Risk/Return Table on 4/18/2013 (T+0)

(T+0) Chang In RUT Price	-40.00	-30.00	-20.00	-10.00	0.00	10.00	20.00	30.00	40.00
RUT Price	861.60	871.60	881.60	891.60	901.60	911.60	921.60	931.60	941.60
Estimated ATM IV	24.00%	23.10%	22.20%	21.40%	20.60%	19.90%	19.20%	18.40%	17.70%
IV Daily VOL	2.99	2.88	2.77	2.67	2.57	2.48	2.40	2.30	2.21
Rf Daily VOL	0.0095	0.0095	0.0095	0.0095	0.0095	0.0095	0.0095	0.0095	0.0095
Delta	29.50	23.99	16.86	8.73	0.24	-7.73	-14.65	-20.00	-23.58
Gamma	-0.46	-0.65	-0.78	-0.85	-0.84	-0.76	-0.62	-0.45	-0.26
Vega	49.90	36.38	25.96	20.50	21.11	27.79	39.51	54.29	70.03
Theta	16.17	23.16	29.21	33.60	35.87	35.80	33.61	29.77	24.88
Rho	-0.72	-0.72	-0.72	-0.72	-0.72	-0.72	-0.72	-0.72	-0.72
Warning Level	-4.00	-4.00	-4.00	-4.00	-4.00	-4.00	-4.00	-4.00	-4.00
Double Diagonal DTRRR	-13.23	-7.96	-4.88	-2.80	-1.17	-2.17	-3.16	-4.13	-5.22
Double Diagonal VTRRR	-4.51	-2.21	-1.20	-0.79	-0.74	-0.94	-1.37	-2.04	-3.03
Double Diagonal RTRRR	-0.0002	-0.0001	-0.0001	-0.0001	-0.0001	-0.0001	-0.0001	-0.0001	-0.0001

The key to the low level of Vega risk per unit of prospective return was the initial Vega/Theta relationship. The initial Vega of the double diagonal was $21.11, which was only a fraction of the initial value of Theta ($35.87). Conversely, for all of the other strategies we have examined, the opening absolute values of Vega were three to four times the corresponding values of Theta.

For the double diagonal strategy, increases or decreases in the price of RUT would have caused Theta to decline and Vega to increase, but the initial value of VTRRR was sufficiently low to ensure a reasonable level of volatility risk per unit of return over nearly the entire spectrum of prospective price changes.

For an instantaneous price change of minus $40 in RUT, the VTRRR of the double diagonal would have fallen to minus 4.51, only slightly beyond the warning threshold. The average VTRRR for all of the other price scenarios (minus $30 to plus $40) would have been minus 1.54, which was well inside the warning level.

Double Diagonal Optimization

For all of the earlier strategies, the VTRRR was higher than we would have preferred, which required us to accept a greater level of Vega exposure than was desirable – or even necessary. For each of these monthly strategies, we discovered that weekly options mitigated much of the excessive Vega risk, without sacrificing potential return. The resulting VTRRRs of the comparable weekly strategies were much lower than the monthly VTRRRs.

The double diagonal spread used a much more direct approach to reducing Vega exposure; it partially hedged Vega risk by integrating positive and negative Vega components of the other income strategies. As a result, there is no incentive for exploring double diagonal spreads constructed from weekly options; the VTRRR for the monthly double diagonal spread was already quite low.

Unfortunately, weekly options did not substantially improve the full range of DTRRRs for the other strategies tested (iron condor, calendar spread, and iron butterfly), nor did the monthly double diagonal strategy. Ideally, we would like to construct a strategy that reduced the magnitude of the DTRRR and the VTRRR over the entire range of prospective price changes. To do so, we will need to use a more direct approach.

11 HYBRID COMBINATIONS

In Chapters 7 through 10, we examined the risk/return ratios for four typical option-income strategies: the iron condor, the calendar spread, the iron butterfly, and the double diagonal. For each strategy, we examined the DTRRRs and VTRRRs over a wide range of prices, which highlighted the strengths and weaknesses of each strategy. While this was enlightening, we do not have to limit ourselves to conventional option-income strategies.

Now that we have these new tools at our disposal, it would be much more efficient to deliberately construct a hybrid strategy that minimizes price and implied volatility risk per unit of return. In other words, we should attempt to identify and employ the option income strategy with the lowest absolute values of DTRRR and VTRRR, in the context of a specific market environment.

I will introduce the concept of formal risk/return optimization in Chapter 13; for now, this chapter will examine a hybrid combination option-income strategy example that was designed using the risk/return ratios in this book. There are countless hybrid strategies that are not combinations of conventional strategies, but to keep this example as simple as possible, the hybrid strategy used in this chapter will be constructed by combining several of the strategies that were described in earlier chapters: specifically two broken-wing butterflies and one calendar spread. If we relaxed this constraint, we could create a much richer set of prospective option-income strategies.

The calendar spread and broken-wing butterfly we examined in Chapters 8 and 9 were designed to stand alone as Delta-neutral option income strategies. Conversely, the broken-wing butterflies and calendar spread used in this chapter are only elements of the hybrid combination and are not intended to function independently as option income strategies.

In fact, the broken-wing butterflies and the calendar spread used to construct the hybrid strategy will be created using out-of-the-money options. Therefore, the OTM butterflies and OTM calendar spread will not be Delta-neutral when examined individually. They will only be Delta-neutral when aggregated into the hybrid combination strategy.

OTM Broken-Wing Put Butterfly

The first sub-component of the hybrid strategy is an OTM broken-wing put butterfly. Note that this is not an iron butterfly; it is a standard butterfly constructed with OTM put options. This is typically how directional broken-wing butterflies are created – with OTM options. Remember that OTM options are typically more liquid, which results in narrower bid-ask spreads and lower transaction costs.

The OTM broken-wing put butterfly component of the hybrid strategy was constructed with the following three positions on April 18, 2013:

+4 RUT 870 MAY 13 Puts
- 8 RUT 855 MAY 13 Puts
+4 RUT 825 MAY 13 Puts

All three put options are out of the money and the number of long positions exactly offsets the number of short positions. However, the spread between the long 870 puts and the short 855 puts (15 points) is narrower than the spread between the short 855 puts and the long 825 puts (30 points). The profit and loss diagram for the resulting OTM broken-wing put butterfly is depicted in Figure 11.1. The percentages are not relevant, because this is only one component of the hybrid strategy, but the profit and loss values for this component expressed in dollars are relevant, as is the overall shape of the diagram in Figure 11.1.

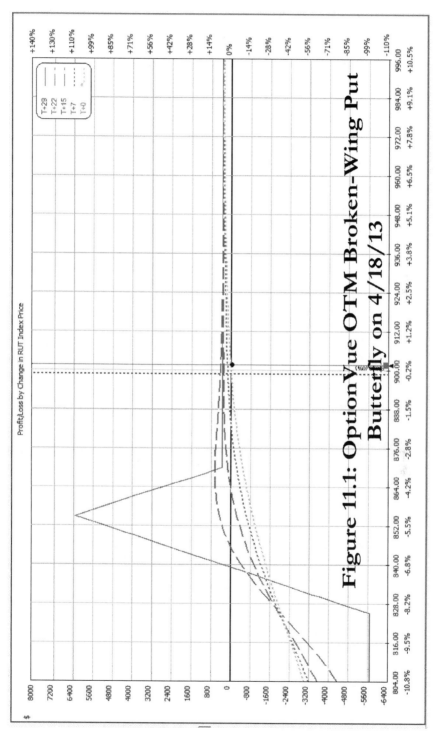

Figure 11.1: OptionVue OTM Broken-Wing Put Butterfly on 4/18/13

The OTM broken-wing put butterfly component would have been profitable at expiration (T+29 line) for any RUT price change greater than minus 7.0%. In addition, the broken-wing put butterfly had positive Theta over a very wide range of RUT prices. How can we determine this from the diagram? The T+19 line is above the T+10 line, which is above the T+0 line. In other words, as time passed, the value of this component of the hybrid strategy would have increased in value.

The long flat region of the diagram is appealing, but this component would still have had positive Delta and negative Vega. In addition, the profit and loss would have dropped off sharply for a large decline in RUT prices. Is there anything we could do to address all of these issues?

OTM Put Calendar Spread

We could add an OTM put calendar spread component to the hybrid strategy. The OTM calendar spread would have negative Delta and positive Vega, which would help offset the Delta and Vega exposure of the OTM broken-wing put butterfly. It would even have positive Theta, at least for a range of possible RUT prices. Finally, the strike prices for the OTM put calendar component could be chosen specifically to mitigate the sharp drop-off that occurred in the OTM put butterfly (see Figure 11.2).

The OTM put calendar spread component of the hybrid strategy was constructed with the following two positions on April 18, 2013:

-1 RUT 850 MAY 13 Puts
+1 RUT 850 JUN 13 Puts

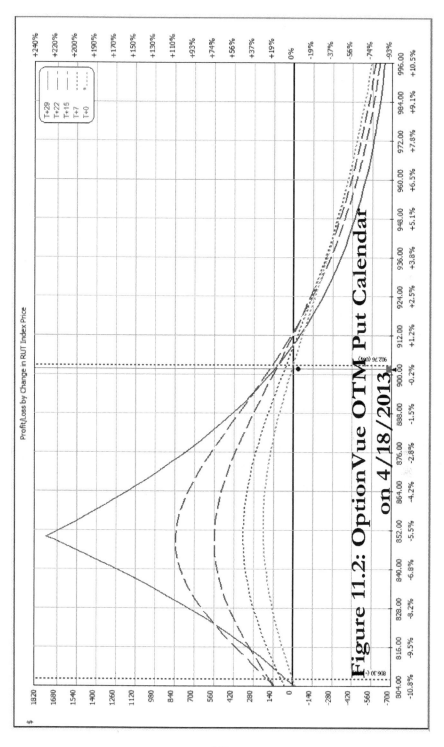

Figure 11.2: OptionVue OTM Put Calendar on 4/18/2013

The combined position of the OTM broken-wing put butterfly and the OTM put calendar spread would not quite have been market-neutral and the calendar spread would have generated a drag on performance for an increase in RUT prices. As a result, we would have needed one final component to complete the hybrid strategy: an OTM broken-wing *call* butterfly.

OTM Broken-Wing Call Butterfly

The OTM broken-wing call butterfly component of the hybrid strategy was constructed with the following three positions on April 18, 2013:

+1 RUT 955 MAY 13 Calls
- 2 RUT 940 MAY 13 Calls
+1 RUT 930 MAY 13 Calls

As was the case for the OTM put butterfly, all three call options would have been out of the money and the number of long call positions would have exactly offset the number of short call positions. The spread between the long 955 calls and the short 940 calls (15 points) is wider than the spread between the short 940 calls and the long 930 calls (10 points). This spread difference produced the unique shape of the broken-wing butterfly in Figure 11.3.

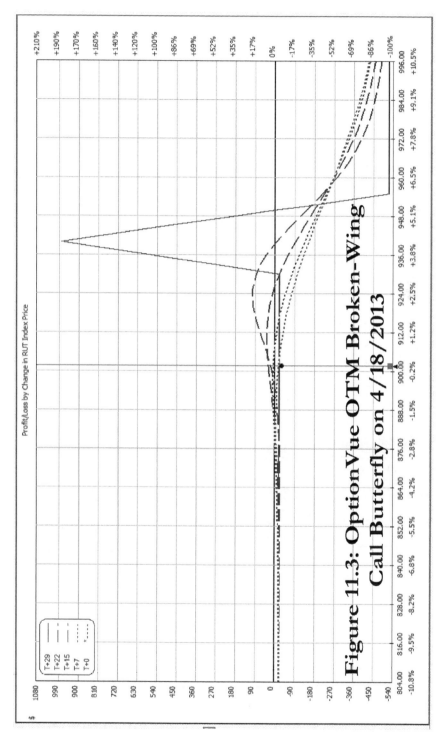

Figure 11.3: OptionVue OTM Broken-Wing Call Butterfly on 4/18/2013

When creating complex positions, it is invaluable to have an analytical platform to experiment with different strategy components and to graph the resulting profit and loss functions. Figure 11.4 is a partial screen capture image from OptionVue's graphical analysis screen for the hybrid combination strategy. The hybrid strategy includes the following three components explained earlier: an OTM broken-wing put butterfly, an OTM put calendar spread, and an OTM broken-wing call butterfly.

There are several important characteristics to note from the hybrid profit and loss function in Figure 11.4. First, the diagram is very flat over a wide range of prices. Unlike the calendar, butterfly, and double diagonal, the hybrid profit and loss function does not have a large peak at the center of the diagram, which also means that it does not fall off as sharply at the extremes.

Instead, the hybrid strategy takes the excess performance from the center of the diagram and spreads it out more evenly. The resulting break-even RUT prices for the hybrid strategy over a holding period of 19 days (T+19 line) would have been approximately $840 (-6.77%) to $940 (+4.25%). The additional break-even price protection on the downside relative to the upside is consistent with the fact that equity prices fall much faster than they rise.

The hybrid strategy also has positive Theta, which is evidenced by the fact that the T+19 line is above the T+10 line, which is above the T+0 line over a wide range of prices. This relationship would have held for RUT prices from approximately $820 (-9.05%) to $960 (+6.48%).

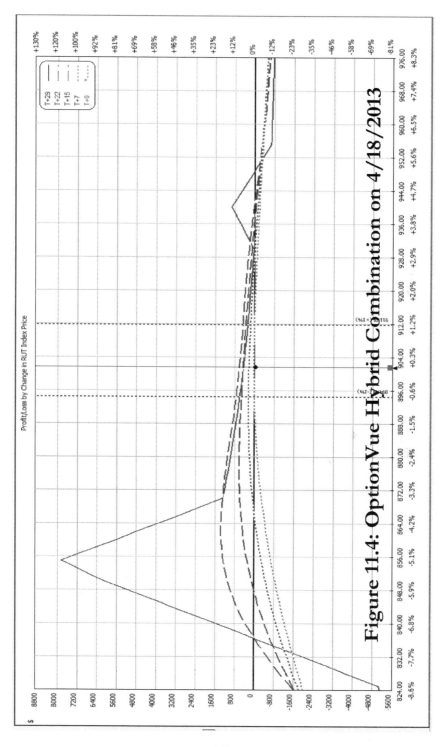

Figure 11.4: OptionVue Hybrid Combination on 4/18/2013

Now that we have evaluated the prospective performance of the hybrid combination strategy, let's review the required transactions before contemplating the entry technique. You will recall that the hybrid strategy included the following three components: an OTM broken-wing put butterfly, an OTM put calendar spread, and an OTM broken-wing call butterfly.

The OTM broken-wing put butterfly component of the hybrid strategy was constructed with the following three positions on April 18, 2013:

+4 RUT 870 MAY 13 Puts

- 8 RUT 855 MAY 13 Puts

+4 RUT 825 MAY 13 Puts

The OTM put calendar spread component of the hybrid strategy was constructed with the following two positions on April 18, 2013:

-1 RUT 850 MAY 13 Puts

+1 RUT 850 JUN 13 Puts

The OTM broken-wing call butterfly component of the hybrid strategy was constructed with the following three positions on April 18, 2013:

+1 RUT 955 MAY 13 Calls

- 2 RUT 940 MAY 13 Calls

+1 RUT 930 MAY 13 Calls

Figure 11.5 is a partial screen capture of OptionVue's RUT matrix on April 18, 2013. All of the component positions are documented in the RUT matrix, as are the per-contract Delta values for a subset of the MAY and JUN options. The OTM broken-wing call butterfly positions are located at the top of the matrix and the OTM broken-wing put butterfly and OTM put calendar positions are located near the bottom of the matrix. According to OptionVue's calculations, the FINRA margin requirements for the hybrid strategy would have been $6,948 (not shown).

Options	MAY <29> (May 17)						JUN <64> (Jun 21)					
960 C	MktPr	MIV	Trade	Ex.Pos	Delta	T.Prem	MktPr	MIV	Trade	Ex.Pos	Delta	T.Prem
955 C	2.08	16.2%		+1	11.0	2.08	6.85	16.1%			21.2	6.85
950 C	2.73	16.4%			13.7	2.73	8.05	16.3%			23.7	8.05
945 C	3.65	16.7%			16.7	3.65	9.45	16.5%			26.4	9.45
940 C	4.60	16.9%		-2	20.1	4.60	11.00	16.7%			29.1	11.00
935 C	5.90	17.3%			23.8	5.90	12.70	17.0%			31.9	12.70
930 C	7.30	17.6%		+1	27.8	7.30	14.60	17.3%			34.8	14.60
925 C	9.00	17.9%			32.0	9.00	16.60	17.5%			37.7	16.60
920 C	11.05	18.4%			36.3	11.05	18.80	17.8%			40.6	18.80
915 C	13.15	18.7%			40.7	13.15	21.15	18.0%			43.6	21.15
910 C	15.55	19.2%			45.1	15.55	23.65	18.3%			46.5	23.65
905 C	18.15	19.5%			49.5	18.15	26.30	18.5%			49.4	26.30
900 C >	20.90	19.8%			53.7	19.30	29.10	18.8%			52.3	27.50
900 P >	21.05	21.5%			-47.1	21.05	30.90	21.1%			-47.0	30.90
895 P	18.95	21.9%			-43.5	18.95	28.90	21.4%			-44.5	28.90
890 P	17.15	22.3%			-40.0	17.15	26.85	21.6%			-42.1	26.85
885 P	15.50	22.8%			-36.6	15.50	25.05	21.9%			-39.7	25.05
880 P	13.95	23.1%			-33.5	13.95	23.30	22.2%			-37.4	23.30
875 P	12.60	23.6%			-30.5	12.60	21.60	22.4%			-35.2	21.60
870 P	11.35	24.0%		+4	-27.7	11.35	20.10	22.7%			-33.1	20.10
865 P	10.20	24.4%			-25.1	10.20	18.70	23.0%			-31.1	18.70
860 P	9.15	24.8%			-22.7	9.15	17.35	23.3%			-29.2	17.35
855 P	8.25	25.3%		-8	-20.5	8.25	16.20	23.7%			-27.3	16.20
850 P	7.45	25.8%		-1	-18.5	7.45	15.00	23.8%		+1	-25.6	15.00
845 P	6.65	26.1%			-16.7	6.65	13.90	24.1%			-23.9	13.90
840 P	5.95	26.5%			-15.0	5.95	12.90	24.5%			-22.3	12.90
835 P	5.35	27.0%			-13.5	5.35	11.95	24.8%			-20.8	11.95
830 P	4.80	27.3%			-12.2	4.80	11.20	25.2%			-19.4	11.20
825 P	4.30	27.7%		+4	-11.0	4.30	10.25	25.3%			-18.1	10.25
Summary												

Figure 11.5: OptionVue Hybrid Matrix

Hybrid Strategy Entry Technique

The main drawbacks of the hypothetical hybrid combination are the complexity and potential costs associated with execution. This hybrid combination was made up of three separate components, which would have required a total of eight different option positions. Unfortunately, spread books on the option exchanges are currently limited to a total of four separate option positions. As a result, it would not currently be possible to enter or exit the hybrid combination strategy using a single limit order, as we were able to do for all of the other option income strategies. That means that we would not be able to avoid market risk when entering the hybrid strategy. That is an unfortunate problem that we cannot avoid.

For this particular hybrid combination, the limit order for the OTM broken-wing put butterfly should be worked first. This component has the greatest number of contracts and is a critical element of the hybrid strategy. Minimizing the transaction costs for the OTM broken-wing put butterfly would have the greatest impact on the overall success of the hybrid combination.

Once filled on that trade, the incomplete hybrid strategy would temporarily be exposed to changes in both price and implied volatility. As a result, the limit order to buy the OTM put calendar spread should be submitted immediately upon getting filled on the OTM put butterfly. The spread order should be set up in advance and ready to submit at the push of a button. Depending on the level of intra-day volatility, it might be necessary to make a slight concession on the limit price of the calendar spread, but it should still be possible to execute the spread *near* the midpoint between the bid and ask prices. It would be important to execute the calendar spread order quickly to hedge most of the outstanding Delta and Vega risk from the put butterfly.

The final OTM broken-wing call butterfly limit order should also be prepared in advance, but the timing of the execution would not be as critical as the calendar spread. Nevertheless, the OTM call butterfly order should be submitted as soon as the calendar spread order was filled. The OTM broken-wing call butterfly only has a small impact on the Greeks, but it is still an important component of the strategy. The hybrid combination would not be complete until all three trades were executed.

Hybrid Strategy Risk/Return Ratios

Figure 11.6 is a graphical summary of the DTRRR and VTRRR for the hybrid combination strategy on April 18, 2013. This chart is comparable to the risk/return ratio strategy charts from prior chapters. The DTRRR is depicted by the dotted line and the VTRRR is represented by the dashed line. Instantaneous price changes of minus $40 to plus $40 are provided in the chart. The hypothetical warning level of minus 4.00 is the horizontal solid line.

The circle in the center of the graph represents the DTRRR on the entry date of the hybrid combination on April 18, 2013. At entry, the initial DTRRR value of minus 0.95 was better than any of the other monthly strategies. For increases in the price of RUT, several of the preceding strategies had well behaved DTRRRs, which eventually crossed the warning level after a $30 (3.3%) increase in the price of RUT.

The DTRRRs of the hybrid combination strategy were even more impressive. They *never* crossed the warning level for any of the prospective RUT price increases ($0 to +$40). The initial level of price risk per unit of return was very low and remained inside the warning level over the entire range of prospective price *increases*.

As was the case with all of the earlier strategies, the price risk relative to the prospective return would have deteriorated much more rapidly for the hybrid strategies had RUT prices declined. Nevertheless, the hybrid strategy would have outperformed all of the previous strategies. An instantaneous $27 decline in the price of RUT would have been required to force the DTRRR of the hybrid combination to penetrate the warning threshold.

The hybrid combination offered far more downside price risk protection than any of the other strategies. A $40 decline in the price of RUT would have caused the DTRRR of the hybrid combination to grow to minus 6.16. While this was beyond the warning threshold, minus 6.16 would have been the lowest level of price risk per unit of return for any of the monthly strategies after the extreme $40 price decline. Only the DTRRR of the iron condor (-7.64) was remotely similar to that of the hybrid for the down $40 price scenario.

The initial DTRRR results of the hybrid strategy are very encouraging. The magnitude of the initial DTRRR was lower than any of the other strategies and the level of price risk per unit of return dominated all of the other strategies over the entire range of prospective price changes: minus $40 to plus $40.

If the DTRRR results for the hybrid strategy were encouraging, then the VTRRR results were truly spectacular. We discovered earlier that the double diagonal was able to hedge some of its Vega exposure by using the positive Vega of the calendar spread to offset some of the negative Vega of the iron butterfly. The hybrid strategy took this concept one step further and attempted to reduce Delta and Vega over a wide range of prospective prices, without sacrificing positive Theta.

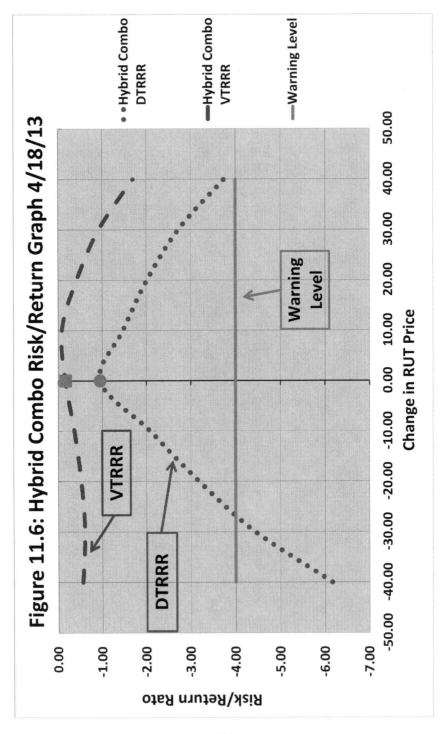

Figure 11.6: Hybrid Combo Risk/Return Graph 4/18/13

As you can see from the risk/return graph in Figure 11.6, the hybrid strategy was very effective in reducing Vega risk per unit of return. The initial VTRRR for the hybrid strategy was minus 0.17, which was a tiny fraction of the VTRRRs of the other monthly option income strategies. Even better, the magnitude of the VTRRR for the hybrid strategy would have remained low; it *never* would have exceeded the warning level for *any* of the prospective price changes: minus $40 to plus $40. In fact, the worst level of Vega risk per unit of return for the hybrid strategy would have been minus 1.70, after a price change of plus $40. Remarkably, the average VTRRR across all prospective price changes would have been only minus 0.59.

How was this possible? The answer is evident in Figure 11.7. The initial Vega of the hybrid strategy was only minus $3.94, which is extremely small, especially when compared to the initial value of Theta: $29.34. The size of Vega would have been manageable over the entire prospective range of prices, which would have kept the VTRRR from penetrating the warning level. Theta would also have remained positive over the entire region.

As discussed earlier, the profit function was relatively flat over a wide distribution of prices. This would have kept Gamma exposure to a minimum. Eventually, large price declines would have caused the DTRRR to penetrate the warning level, but the hybrid strategy would have generated lower levels of risk per unit of return than any of the other strategies.

The resulting price and implied volatility risks per unit of return for the hybrid strategy were superior to all of the other monthly income strategies – because that was the way the hybrid strategy was designed.

Figure 11.7: Hybrid Combination Risk/Return Table on 4/18/2013 (T+0)

(T+0) Chang In RUT Price	-40.00	-30.00	-20.00	-10.00	0.00	10.00	20.00	30.00	40.00
RUT Price	861.60	871.60	881.60	891.60	901.60	911.60	921.60	931.60	941.60
Estimated ATM IV	24.00%	23.10%	22.20%	21.40%	20.60%	19.90%	19.20%	18.40%	17.70%
IV Daily VOL	2.99	2.88	2.77	2.67	2.57	2.48	2.40	2.30	2.21
Rf Daily VOL	0.0095	0.0095	0.0095	0.0095	0.0095	0.0095	0.0095	0.0095	0.0095
Delta	27.04	19.64	12.77	6.28	0.68	-3.69	-6.52	-8.15	-9.22
Gamma	-0.76	-0.71	-0.67	-0.62	-0.50	-0.38	-0.20	-0.13	-0.08
Vega	-13.36	-15.50	-13.57	-9.30	-3.94	1.85	7.89	14.46	21.07
Theta	35.11	36.31	35.24	32.68	29.34	25.65	21.78	17.56	13.32
Rho	-22.65	-22.65	-22.65	-22.65	-22.65	-22.65	-22.65	-22.65	-22.65
Warning Level	-4.00	-4.00	-4.00	-4.00	-4.00	-4.00	-4.00	-4.00	-4.00
Hybrid Combo DTRRR	-6.16	-4.43	-3.18	-2.08	-0.95	-1.48	-2.02	-2.73	-3.75
Hybrid Combo VTRRR	-0.56	-0.60	-0.52	-0.37	-0.17	-0.09	-0.42	-0.92	-1.70
Hybrid Combo RTRRR	-0.0030	-0.0029	-0.0030	-0.0032	-0.0036	-0.0041	-0.0048	-0.0060	-0.0079

Hybrid Strategy Optimization

In Chapters 7 through 10, we explored different ways to improve upon each of the monthly option income strategies. That is not necessary in this chapter. The hybrid strategy introduced in this chapter was created specifically to reduce the levels of risk per unit return. The resulting hybrid strategy had consistent results over a wide range of prices and generated far lower levels of risk per unit of return than any of the conventional option income strategies introduced in Chapters 7-10.

That should be no surprise. The hybrid strategy was created using an iterative process of evaluating the Greeks and the resulting DTRRR and VTRRR values with the explicit goals of minimizing risk and maximizing prospective return. The traditional strategies in Chapters 7-10 were Delta-balanced; but the risk/return ratios were not used directly to optimize these strategies.

The hybrid candidates considered for inclusion in this chapter were limited to those that could be constructed by combining the strategies from Chapters 7 - 10. If we were to relax this constraint, we could create a much richer set of prospective option-income strategies, which could lower our levels of risk per unit of return even further. This would require a more formal method of strategy optimization, which will be addressed in Chapter 13.

Before exploring optimization and other practical considerations, Chapter 12 will summarize the risk/return ratios for all of the strategies we have examined thus far – using both graphical and tabular formats.

12 STRATEGY SUMMARY

In Chapters 7 through 11, we reviewed the risk and return characteristics of each of the option income strategies individually, but it is much easier to compare and contrast the strategies by examining their risk/return ratios collectively as a group. Now that we have all of the required data, that will be our goal in Chapter 12.

Strategy Summary Risk/Return Ratios

Figure 12.1 is a table summarizing the DTRRRs for each of the strategies across the same range of prospective RUT price changes that we used in previous chapters: minus $40 to plus $40, in $10 increments. Each column reports the DTRRRs for each strategy for the given RUT price level.

The values in the first column equal the average DTRRRs for each strategy, calculated across all nine possible price levels. Remember that DTRRRs are always negative, so we prefer strategy DTRRRs to have as small an absolute value as possible. The strategies are listed from the lowest average absolute value of DTRRR to the highest (least negative to most negative). As a result, the strategy with the lowest level of price risk per unit of return is at the top (best) and the strategy with the highest level of price risk per unit of return is at the bottom (worst).

Here are the average DTRRR strategy results from best to worst: 1) hybrid combination, 2) iron condor, 3) calendar spread, 4) double diagonal, and 5) iron butterfly. It should be no surprise that the hybrid combination had the lowest average level of price risk per unit of return. In fact, it had the lowest level of price risk per unit of return at every price level. It dominated the other monthly strategies. Unlike the conventional option income strategies, the hybrid strategy was specifically designed to minimize the DTRRR across a wide range of prospective price changes.

The DTRRR results for the iron condor were respectable. The average DTRRR for the iron condor was minus 4.02, which was reasonably close to the average DTRRR for the hybrid combination (-2.98). Why did the iron condor outperform the other conventional strategies? Because its profit and loss function was relatively flat by comparison. The calendar spread, double diagonal, and iron butterfly all have prominent peaked regions at the center of their profit and loss functions. As a result, price risk tends to increase more dramatically for these strategies at the extremes, which adversely affects their DTRRRs.

The average DTRRRs for the remaining strategies were minus 4.87 for the calendar spread, minus 4.97 for the double diagonal, and an atrocious minus 10.27 for the iron butterfly. The DTRRRs deteriorated more rapidly to the downside for all of the strategies. This is due to the fact that volatility increases when equity prices decline, which magnifies the Delta and Gamma Effects. The relative DTRRRs for the calendar spread, the double diagonal, and the iron butterfly were far worse than those of the iron condor or the hybrid combination strategy. The downside DTRRRs of the iron butterfly were especially troubling.

Through my optimization research, I discovered that using systematic filters to avoid butterfly trades when the market has an elevated risk of a pullback increases the return and reduces the risk of the broken-wing iron butterfly strategy. The directional disparity in the butterfly DTRRRs supports this conclusion. Monthly broken-wing iron butterfly campaigns tend to perform best during creeping uptrends, as volatility gradually declines. Despite being Delta-neutral at inception, there is a surprising directional element to the broken-wing iron butterfly strategy.

It is encouraging that the DTRRRs in Figure 12.1 support the conclusions from my optimization research and are consistent with the insights gained from my trading experience, but the main benefit of these new tools is their ability to design option income strategies that offer the lowest level of risk per unit of return in any market environment. The specific hybrid combination strategy outlined in this chapter is an excellent example of what can be accomplished using risk/return ratios, but it is only one of many possible hybrid combination strategies that lower the level of risk per unit of return.

Change In RUT Price	Average	-40.00	-30.00	-20.00	-10.00	0.00	10.00	20.00	30.00	40.00
RUT Price		861.60	871.60	881.60	891.60	901.60	911.60	921.60	931.60	941.60
Warning Level	-4.00	-4.00	-4.00	-4.00	-4.00	-4.00	-4.00	-4.00	-4.00	-4.00
Hybrid Combo DTRRR	-2.98	-6.16	-4.43	-3.18	-2.08	-0.95	-1.48	-2.02	-2.73	-3.75
Iron Condor DTRRR	-4.02	-7.64	-5.44	-3.71	-2.35	-1.13	-2.22	-3.36	-4.49	-5.80
Calendar DTRRR	-4.87	-13.30	-7.89	-4.83	-2.75	-1.15	-2.19	-3.09	-3.92	-4.68
Double Diagonal DTRRR	-4.97	-13.23	-7.96	-4.88	-2.80	-1.17	-2.17	-3.16	-4.13	-5.22
Iron Butterfly DTRRR	-10.27	-50.44	-14.69	-7.30	-3.81	-1.60	-2.23	-3.18	-4.08	-5.10

Figure 12.1: All Strategies DTRRR Table on 4/18/2013 (T+0)

173

Figure 12.2 is a graphical summary of the DTRRR for all of the option income strategies we have examined. This chart is comparable to the risk/return ratio strategy charts from prior chapters, except that all of the strategies are included on the same chart. The minimum risk/return value on the y-axis in Figure 12.2 was capped at minus 10 to make it easier to interpret the remaining chart values. As you can see from the table in Figure 12.1, several of the DTRRR values would have been below minus 10.

As was the case in the preceeding summary table, the strategies are listed from best to worst. The strategies with the least negative DTRRRs offer the lowest level of risk per unit of return and appear near the top of the chart. The DTRRRs for the hybrid combination are illustrated with the small-dashed line (top). Again, the hybrid combination easily dominates all of the other strategies, offering the lowest level of risk per unit of return across the entire range of prospective price changes.

The downside risks for each strategy are evident in the diagram as are the prospective price levels where the DTRRRs would have penetrated the hypothetical warning level. The values from the table in Figure 12.1 were used to generate the graph in Figure 12.2, but some relationships are easier to identify graphically, which is why both the summary table and the graph were included.

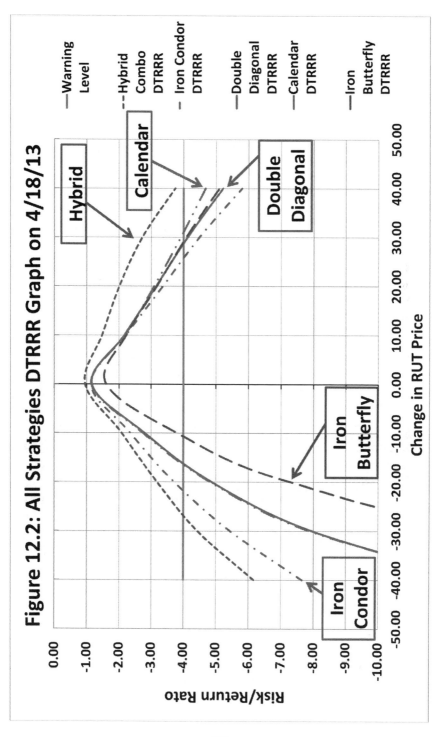

Figure 12.2: All Strategies DTRRR Graph on 4/18/13

Figure 12.3 is a table summarizing the VTRRRs for each of the strategies, for instantaneous RUT price changes of minus $40 to plus $40. Each column represents the VTRRRs for the given RUT price level. Each row includes the VTRRRs for a specific strategy.

The values in the first column represent the average VTRRRs for each strategy calculated across all nine possible price levels. The strategies are listed from the lowest average absolute value of VTRRR to the highest (least negative to most negative). As a result, the strategy with the lowest level of implied volatility risk per unit of return is at the top (best) and the strategy with the highest level of implied volatility risk per unit of return is at the bottom (worst).

Here are the average VTRRR strategy results from best to worst: 1) hybrid combination, 2) double diagonal, 3) iron condor, 4) iron butterfly, and 5) calendar spread. Again, it should be no surprise that the hybrid combination had the lowest average level of implied volatility risk per unit of return. It also had the lowest level of implied volatility risk per unit of return at every price level. The average VTRRR for the hybrid combination strategy was a remarkable minus 0.59. This illustrates how effective the risk/return ratios can be when used to construct market-neutral option income strategies.

The VTRRR results for the double diagonal were quite reasonable as well. The average VTRRR for the double diagonal was only minus 1.87, which was worse than the average VTRRR for the hybrid combination (-0.59), but far better than the average VTRRRs of the other strategies. The double diagonal strategy was able to reduce the level of implied volatility risk per unit of return by hedging some of its Vega exposure with offsetting strategy components.

The iron condor finished in third place with an average VTRRR of minus 3.47, which was significantly worse than the average VTRRRs of the hybrid combination and double diagonal, but better than the average VTRRR of the iron butterfly (-4.74) and considerably better than the average VTRRR of the calendar spread (-7.57).

Figure 12.3: All Strategies VTRRR Table on 4/18/2013 (T+0)

Change In RUT Price	-40.00	-30.00	-20.00	-10.00	0.00	10.00	20.00	30.00	40.00	Average
RUT Price	861.60	871.60	881.60	891.60	901.60	911.60	921.60	931.60	941.60	Warning Level
Hybrid Combo VTRRR	-0.56	-0.60	-0.52	-0.37	-0.17	-0.09	-0.42	-0.92	-1.70	-0.59
Double Diagonal VTRRR	-4.51	-2.21	-1.20	-0.79	-0.74	-0.94	-1.37	-2.04	-3.03	-1.87
Iron Condor VTRRR	-4.07	-3.86	-3.71	-3.61	-3.51	-3.41	-3.27	-3.05	-2.77	-3.47
Iron Butterfly VTRRR	-11.90	-6.20	-4.98	-4.31	-3.86	-3.48	-3.10	-2.66	-2.16	-4.74
Calendar VTRRR	-17.45	-10.62	-7.42	-5.81	-5.04	-4.84	-5.03	-5.54	-6.37	-7.57

Warning Level: -4.00 across all columns.

Unlike the hybrid combination and the double diagonal, the iron condor and iron butterfly do not directly or indirectly hedge implied volatility risk, which explains why their VTRRRs were elevated. The VTRRRs of the iron butterfly were significantly worse than those of the iron condor, but only on the downside. As was the case with the DTRRRs of the iron butterfly, the VTRRRs would have quickly penetrated the warning threshold had RUT prices declined. This reinforces the earlier observation that monthly broken-wing iron butterfly campaigns tend to perform best during docile uptrends.

The VTRRRs of the calendar spread were outside the warning threshold at every price level, even at inception of the trade. Monthly calendar spreads may be Delta-neutral, but they are not market-neutral. They incur excessive levels of implied volatility risk per unit of return and are not competitive with other option income strategies. Monthly calendar spreads are not market-neutral. The excessive VTRRRs make this quite clear.

Figure 12.4 is a graphical summary of the VTRRR for all of the option income strategies. The chart is comparable to the risk/return ratio strategy charts from prior chapters, except that all of the strategies are included on the same chart. As was the case with the DTRRR summary chart, the minimum risk/return value on the y-axis in Figure 12.4 was capped at minus 10 to make it easier to interpret the remaining chart values. The iron butterfly and calendar spread both had VTRRR values blow minus 10 that are not visible on the chart.

The strategies are listed from best to worst. The strategies with the least negative VTRRRs offer the lowest level of risk per unit of return and appear near the top of the chart. The VTRRRs for the hybrid combination are illustrated with the small-dashed line (top). As was the case with the DTRRRs, the hybrid combination dominates all of the other strategies, offering the lowest level of risk per unit of return across the entire range of prospective price changes.

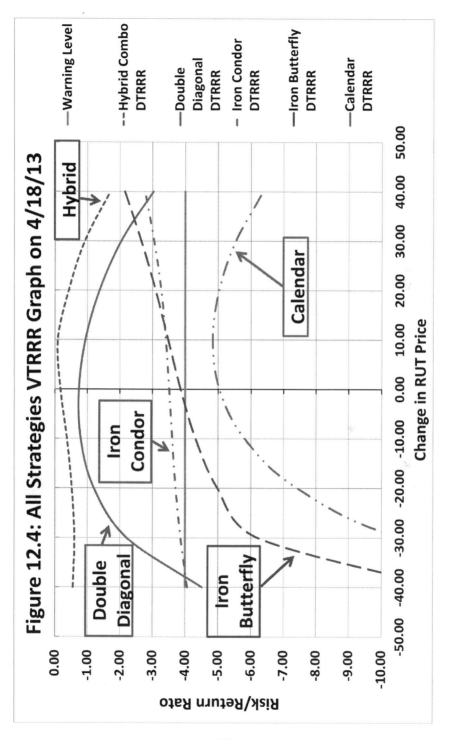

Figure 12.4: All Strategies VTRRR Graph on 4/18/13

The graphic representation of the VTRRRs highlights the risk/return relationships for all of the strategies in a single image. The outstanding performance of the hybrid strategy and the appalling risk/return characteristics of the monthly calendar spread are obvious in the chart. The downside risks for the iron butterfly and calendar spread strategy are evident in the diagram. The prospective price levels where the VTRRRs would have penetrated the hypothetical warning level are also important to note for each strategy.

This chapter compared and contrasted the risk/return ratios for all of the strategies that we examined in Chapters 7 through 11. The iron condor, calendar spread, iron butterfly and double diagonal are all conventional option income strategies that are widely used by option traders. The hybrid strategy was constructed by combining two broken-wing butterflies and one calendar spread, but the combination was not random.

The hybrid strategy was created using an iterative process of evaluating the Greeks and the resulting DTRRR and VTRRR values with the explicit goals of minimizing risk and maximizing prospective return. The hybrid results were promising, but the manual process of creating the hybrid strategy was rather cumbersome and there are countless possible hybrid combination strategies that could potentially lower the level of risk per unit of return even further. The next and final chapter will introduce a more formal method of strategy optimization, but will first expose several factors that affect the application of risk/return ratios in practice.

13 PRACTICAL CONSIDERATIONS

In 1973, Fischer Black and Myron Scholes developed the Black-Scholes Option Pricing Model (BSOPM), which was based on several assumptions, including a stochastic or random process that described probabilistically how the price of the underlying security could evolve over time. The original formulas for Delta, Gamma, Vega, Theta, and Rho were all derived from the BSOPM using stochastic calculus, which means that they are dependent on the validity of the same BSOPM assumptions, including the accuracy of the inherent stochastic process.

The BSOPM was revolutionary, but it is widely known and has been verified empirically that the theoretical BSOPM assumptions are not valid in practice and that actual price distributions are inconsistent with the assumed stochastic process.

The construction of every option income strategy is based on the Greeks, as are all of the risk/return ratios. If the values of the Greeks were inaccurate, then our option income strategies would not be market-neutral, we would incur more risk than expected, and the ability of the DTRRR, VTRRR, and RTRRR to accurately quantify the risk and return characteristics of our strategies would be adversely affected.

True Delta and True Gamma

Delta measures the rate of change in the value of an option or an option strategy with respect to an instantaneous change in the price of the underlying security. In addition, the conventional definition of Delta assumes that when the price of the underlying security changes, all of the other variables will remain constant, including implied volatility.

Unfortunately, changes in the price of an underlying security result in changes in the implied volatility of its options. In other words, changes in price and implied volatility are not independent. This violates one of the key assumptions used to calculate Delta, which means that traditional calculations of Delta are biased and do not accurately reflect how option prices actually change in response to changes in the price of an underlying security.

While the relationship between changes in price and implied volatility varies across securities and over time, this relationship can be modeled with a reasonable degree of accuracy. For equity options, changes in the price of the underlying security are inversely related to changes in implied volatility. When equity prices rise, the implied volatility of equity options will fall and vice versa. OptionVue calls this relationship the "constant elasticity of volatility" or CEV, which it calculates individually for every underlying security.

CEV goes a long way toward capturing the relationship between the price and implied volatility, but there is one more important volatility-related factor that we need to consider – the vertical skew. We examined the vertical skew in Chapter 1 and again in Chapter 7. The vertical skew exposes the equity market's implicit assumption that near-term price declines will be larger and more dramatic than near-term price increases. The asymmetrical expected price changes are reflected in the pattern of implied volatilities across strike prices.

OptionVue's vertical skew graph, which was portrayed in Figure 1.7, depicted the asymmetrical volatility pattern in RUT options. The implied volatility line in Figure 1.7 is downward sloping, indicating a higher level of implied volatility for RUT options with low strike prices and a lower level of implied volatility for RUT options with high strike prices. Why is this important?

When equity prices change, not only does that cause implied volatilities of equity options to change (due to CEV), but there is also a secondary effect as each individual option moves up or down the vertical skew curve. A hypothetical example should help clarify these relationships.

Let's assume we own an at-the-money put option on RUT, the current price of RUT is $900, and the strike price of our put option is also $900. Furthermore, let's assume that the annualized implied volatility of our put option is 20%. If the RUT price declined instantaneously from $900 to $860, how and why would the implied volatility of our put option change?

The first effect would be due to CEV. The $40 decrease in the price of RUT would cause the implied volatility of all RUT options to increase. Let's assume that the CEV effect of a $40 price decline would cause the implied volatility of our put option to increase by 4%, from 20% to 24%.

Now we need to consider the effect of moving down the vertical skew curve. Our original put option was an at-the-money option. However, after the $40 decline in the price of RUT, the $900 strike price of our put option would now be $40 above the new RUT price of $860, which means the implied volatility of our put option would decline as it moved down the vertical skew curve. Remember that equity options with high strike prices have lower implied volatilities than equity options with low strike prices and our put option would now have a high strike price. Let's assume the effect of moving down the skew curve would have *reduced* the implied volatility of our formerly ATM put option by 2%.

The net effect of the $40 price decline on the implied volatility of our $900 put option would have been an increase of 2%: plus 4% from CEV and minus 2% from moving down the vertical skew curve. The traditional Delta calculation assumes that implied volatility remains constant as the price of the underlying security changes, but that is not the case. In this example, implied volatility would have increased by 2%, which would have had a significant impact on the price of our put option.

Instead of assuming that volatility remains constant as prices change, OptionVue calculates "true Delta," which includes the expected change in implied volatility due to the combined effects of CEV and the volatility skew on the price of all options. The resulting true Delta calculations incorporate the CEV and volatility skew of each individual security, estimated at the time of the analysis. The resulting true Delta calculations automatically adapt to changes in CEV and the vertical skew and provide much more accurate and realistic estimates of option price sensitivity.

Similarly, Gamma measures the rate of change in the Delta with respect to an instantaneous change in the price of the underlying security. Unfortunately, traditional calculations of Gamma have the same deficiencies as traditional calculations of Delta. Specifically, the standard Gamma calculation assumes that implied volatility remains constant. To correct this bias, OptionVue also calculates "true Gamma," which includes the expected change in implied volatility due to the combined effects of CEV and the vertical volatility skew.

All of the strategy examples in this book use OptionVue's true Delta and true Gamma calculations. Other vendors or brokers may or may not provide comparable estimates of true Delta and true Gamma. Traditional measures of Delta and Gamma are biased and do not reflect the actual price behavior of options. Using these traditional measures of Delta and Gamma could compromise your ability to effectively construct and manage option income strategies. Please ensure that your Delta and Gamma calculations incorporate the expected changes in implied volatility.

True Vega and True Theta

Just as CEV and the vertical skew affect the calculation of Delta and Gamma, the horizontal skew affects the calculation of Vega and Theta. Vega measures the rate of change in the value of an option or an option strategy with respect to an instantaneous change in implied volatility. The traditional Vega calculation assumes that all implied volatilities change by a constant amount, regardless of the amount of time remaining until option expiration. Empirical evidence directly contradicts this assumption.

As explained in Chapter 1, the term-structure of implied volatilities reflects the market's expectations regarding the future level of volatility. Volatility is assumed to be mean-reverting. When volatility is low (below normal), the term structure of implied volatilities will be upward-sloping. In other words, when volatility is below normal, the market assumes that it will return to normal (increase) over time. In this environment, longer-dated options will have higher implied volatilities than shorter-dated options.

The opposite is true when volatility is high. When volatility is above normal, the term structure of volatilities will typically be downward sloping; the market assumes that volatility will return to normal over time. In this high volatility environment, longer-dated options will usually have lower implied volatilities than shorter-dated options.

When we graph all of the historical term structures of volatility over an extended period, the effects of mean-reversion create the shape of a volatility cone (see Figure 1.8), which reveals that the implied volatility of near-term options moves more than the implied volatility of long-term options.

For example, if the implied volatility of a 30-day option increased by 1%, the implied volatility of a 7-day option would change by far more than 1% and the implied volatility of a 60-day option would change by less than 1%. This means that any traditional Vega calculation involving options with different expiration dates (calendar spreads, double diagonals, and hybrids) would overstate the expected impact of a change in implied volatility on long-term options relative to near-term options. Therefore, the traditional Vega calculation is biased and inconsistent with empirical evidence.

Fortunately, the relative volatilities across the entire term-structure of volatilities are quantifiable. As a result, instead of using a traditional Vega calculation that incorrectly assumes that all implied volatilities change by the same amount, we could use relative volatility factors to calculate a weighted or "true Vega" calculation.

I recommend using a true Vega calculation that would estimate the effect of a 1% increase in the 30-day implied volatility on the value of all options, which would imply larger changes in implied volatility for options with fewer than 30 days remaining until expiration and smaller changes in implied volatility for options with more than 30 days remaining until expiration. The relative volatility factors or multipliers used in the true Vega calculation would be determined directly from the recent historical data for each individual security.

The term structure of implied volatilities also affects Theta. Theta measures the rate of change in the value of an option or option strategy as a function of the passage of time. Again, the traditional calculation of Theta assumes that all other variables remain constant, including implied volatility and the price of the underlying security. The persistent nature of the term structure of volatilities appears to contradict this assumption.

If the term structure of volatilities and the price of the underlying security were to remain unchanged from one day to the next, as options aged, they would roll up or down the term structure of volatilities. Specifically, if the term structure of implied volatilities were positively sloped, implied volatilities would decline in a predictable way as options aged. Conversely, if the term structure of implied volatilities were negatively sloped, implied volatilities would increase with the passage of time. Instead of incorrectly assuming that implied volatilities remain constant over time, we should use a "true Theta" calculation that incorporates the actual term structure of volatilities for each individual security.

As I write this in 2014, the OptionVue software currently incorporates the vertical and horizontal volatility skews when calculating projected option prices and strategy values, but it does not currently include these effects in a true Vega or true Theta calculation. I have suggested both of these enhancements to the management at OptionVue and ideally we will see these improvements in a future release.

I am not aware of any commercially available option analytical platform that currently offers true Delta, true Gamma, true Vega, and true Theta calculations, but the field is evolving rapidly and it is only a matter of time. Obviously true Greek calculations are more accurate and more representative of actual option price movements than traditional Greeks; therefore, true Greeks should be used to manage option income strategies and to calculate risk/return ratios whenever possible.

Historical Strategy Optimization

Before introducing a more formal method of using risk/return ratios to construct option income strategies, it is important to recognize that the term optimization has several different meanings when applied to strategy development. Normally, when I refer to strategy optimization, I mean optimizing a set of parameters that describe a set of objective entry and exit rules that deliver the best results over a historical test period, which are confirmed by comparable results on out-of-sample data.

As a rule, I do not trade strategies unless they demonstrate a significant advantage in back and forward testing. In addition, there must be some rationale or premise that explains why the market inefficiency exists and why it will persist in the future.

Unfortunately, backtesting option strategies has always been an extremely challenging and time consuming process. I recently developed a way to systematically test and optimize parameters for option strategies. Historical option data is notoriously inaccurate and is not readily available. OptionVue does provide reliable historical data and a manual backtesting feature, but it is not automated. As a result, I wrote the code in AMIBroker to simulate historical option pricing for option strategies.

I needed accurate theoretical pricing, so I incorporated the vertical and horizontal volatility skews when pricing the strategies. This type of strategy optimization uses historical data and can only be used to identify the optimal entry and exit rules for conventional option income strategies, ones that can be completely defined using one or more structural parameters. For example, it is possible to completely describe a particular iron butterfly by specifying the width of the strikes as a function of the directional implied volatilities.

Unfortunately, it is not possible to use a similar method to describe hybrid strategies, which means that we cannot use historical data to optimize the parameters of a particular hybrid strategy over time. The purpose of creating a hybrid strategy was to minimize price and implied volatility risk and maximize the potential return from Theta in *a specific environment for a specific underlying security.* By definition, the optimal hybrid strategy would change over time, as the market environment changed. While we cannot create a single hybrid strategy that would offer the lowest level of risk per unit of return in every environment, we can attempt to identify the optimal hybrid strategy in a specific market environment.

Hybrid Strategy Optimization

Optimization is a complex subject. The following material does not contain complicated mathematical formulas or detailed descriptions of optimization algorithms or solution methods. Instead, it provides an introduction to a formal optimization process and how that process could be used to identify the best possible option income candidate in a particular environment.

Implementing a formal optimization approach would not be a trivial exercise. However, the process could be automated using tools such as Excel in conjunction with optimization software. Once automated, solving for the optimal hybrid strategy would be as simple as pushing a button. Even if you decide not to use a formal optimization approach in your own investment process, the following concepts should enhance your understanding of designing option income strategies.

Adjustable Variables

There are several elements that we need to consider when using a formal optimization process to identify the best possible hybrid candidate: the variables, the objective function, the constraints, and the optimization platform. The variables are the values that are adjusted in an attempt to identify the optimal solution.

We could use one variable for each option; the value of each variable would represent the number of contracts for a given option in the final solution. Positive values would indicate long positions and negative values would denote short positions. If we had 100 different option candidates to choose from, each with different strike prices and expiration dates, we would need 100 unique adjustable variables. While this approach is intuitive, there is a more flexible set of variables that should be used in practice.

To account for transaction costs, we would actually need four variables for each option candidate. In the preceding example, if we had 100 different option candidates, we would need 400 variables, but only 200 would be adjustable. How would this work?

For each option, we would need variables to represent the number of contracts held before optimization, the number of option contracts purchased during optimization, the number of option contracts sold during optimization, and the number of contracts held after optimization. The number of contracts held before optimization would be known and would not be an adjustable variable.

If we were designing an optimal hybrid strategy from scratch, the beginning values would be zero for every option candidate. However, we could also use this approach to optimize existing hybrid strategies, which would identify the best possible adjustment transactions for an existing strategy in a particular market environment.

The two adjustable variables for each option candidate would be the number of contracts purchased and the number of contracts sold during optimization. The final variable for each candidate would be the final number of option contracts held after optimization. This variable would not be adjustable; it would be determined by the values of the first three variables. The final number of contracts held after optimization would equal the number of contracts held before optimization, plus the number of contracts purchased, minus the number of contracts sold.

This is obviously more complicated than the single variable approach, so how would this help us? First, we ultimately need to know the number of contracts to buy or sell for each option, which would be far easier to determine if we had specific variables for purchases and sales. This would be especially helpful if we were optimizing an existing strategy and already held positions in several different options.

While having the optimization solution identify the number of contracts to buy or sell would be helpful, the primary reason for using separate variables for purchases and sales would be to facilitate the inclusion of transaction costs in the optimization process. In other words, we could penalize our solution for the expected transaction costs incurred through purchases and sales. This would allow us to identify the best possible hybrid solution, net of expected transaction costs. The dollar amount of transaction costs would be a function of the number of contracts purchased or sold and would obviously vary for different prospective solutions.

Objective Function

The idea of penalizing prospective solutions for transaction costs raises the issue of the objective function. What would be our objective, or more specifically, what function or formula would we be trying to maximize or minimize? There is no single best answer that would meet the needs of every trader. As a result, I will offer a number of possible elements that could be included individually or collectively in an objective function.

Since the title of this book is *Option Strategy Risk/Return Ratios*, let's start there. The objective function could be as simple as maximizing the sum of DTRRR, VTRRR, and RTRRR. Why maximize? Remember that all of the preceding risk/return ratios are negative by definition. Maximizing the sum of DTRRR, VTRRR, and RTRRR would identify the hybrid solution with the *least negative* (or maximum) value of DTRRR + VTRRR + RTRRR.

This is a great start, but it would only identify the hybrid strategy with the best risk/return ratios at a specific price level. In the earlier chapters, we discovered that knowing the values of DTRRR and

VTRRR for a range of prospective prices was instrumental in identifying the most robust option income strategies.

We could use the same approach here. Instead of maximizing the current value of DTRRR + VTRRR + RTRRR, we could maximize the sum of the risk/return ratios across a range of prospective prices. If we did so, it would probably not make sense to assign an equal weight to the risk/return ratios for each prospective price level. The probability of RUT increasing or decreasing by $40 is lower than the probability of RUT remaining at or near the current price level. As a result, we could assign a weight to the risk/return ratios at each price level based on a simple normal or lognormal probability distribution. The resulting objective function would maximize the probability-weighed sum of DTRRR, VTRRR, and RTRRR across a range of prospective price levels.

Calculating the risk/return ratios at the initial price level would be straightforward, since the values of the Greeks would be readily available. Calculating the risk return ratios at other price levels would require modeling work. However, once completed, these values could be calculated automatically for all future optimizations.

While maximizing the probability-weighted sum of the risk/return ratios is appealing, it would be difficult to integrate the expected transaction costs directly into this objective function. The risk/return ratios would be expressed in dollars of risk per dollars of return, but transaction costs would be expressed in dollars. The units would be inconsistent and we could not simply subtract the expected level of transaction costs from the sum of the probability-weighted risk/return ratios.

However, instead of using the risk/return ratios directly in the objective function, we could use their components instead: the Delta Effect, the Gamma Effect, the Vega Effect, the Rho Effect, and the Theta Effect. All of these Greek Effects are expressed in dollars, which would be consistent with the units used to measure transaction costs.

The resulting objective function would include the sum of the probability weighed Delta, Gamma, Vega, Rho, and Theta Effects for a range of prospective prices and the expected round-trip transaction costs for implementing the strategy. The Delta, Gamma, Vega, and Rho Effects would all be negative, as would the expected transaction costs. The Theta Effect would be positive. We would still be interested in maximizing this function.

This objective function would work well, but we could go even further. In addition to the Greek Effects, which are forward-looking, we could also include expected changes in the value of the strategy in the objective function. The expected changes in the value of the strategy could also be calculated over a range of prospective prices and probability weighted. The resulting objective function would then include the probability-weighted performance of the strategy looking backward, and the probability-weighed expected performance looking forward, net of transaction costs.

Finally, if we really wanted to get creative, we could even include the relative value of each of the option candidates in our objective function. Undervalued options would have positive values and overvalued options would have negative values. Any or all of the preceding components could be included in an objective function.

OptionVue provides some of this information, including the initial Greeks and relative values for every option in the matrix. This information can be downloaded by the user and used as input data in the optimization process. I have used modeling techniques to estimate the remaining option values, Greeks, and risk/return ratios for additional price levels, which allows me to use objective functions with any or all of the elements introduced in this section.

Constraints

Once we have decided upon a specific objective function and calculated or downloaded the required input data, we need to define constraints, which will limit the range of acceptable solutions. Optimizers are very powerful (and very sneaky) and are quite adept at exploiting missing constraints to come up with some rather original, but impractical solutions. As a result, we need to specify constraints to ensure the resulting optimal strategy satisfies all of our requirements.

There are many different types of constraints. Let's start with structural constraints. We already touched on one structural constraint earlier when we examined the four variables that were required to incorporate transaction costs. You will recall that the final number of contracts held after optimization would equal the number of contracts held before optimization, plus the number of contracts purchased, minus the number of contracts sold. A constraint is simply a formula, specified as an equality or an inequality. In this case, the formula might look like this:

Beginning + Purchases – Sales = Ending

This is an example of a structural constraint. In fact, we would need to include one of these constraints for every option candidate. If we had 100 candidates, we would need 100 such constraints. While this type of constraint seems obvious, it is not obvious to the optimizer. The optimizer must be told explicitly about every relationship or limitation, regardless how rudimentary.

This might seem like a daunting task, but there is some good news. We only have to set up the objective function and constraints once. We could then use the same problem definition with different data sets (different variables) to solve for the optimal hybrid strategy in any future or past environment. In addition, even if we make a mistake and overlook an important constraint, we should discover the mistake the first time we run the optimizer with actual data. The solution would typically be so extreme that we would instantly recognize there was an error in the problem specification.

For our specific optimization problem, we would need some additional structural constraints. First, the Gamma of the optimal strategy must be negative. This constraint might seem odd on the surface, but we are interested in identifying the optimal option income strategy and all option income strategies have negative Gamma. If we did not specify this constraint, the optimizer would find a solution, but it might not be an option income strategy.

We would also implement a corresponding constraint that Theta must be positive, but we could go even further and force the Theta of a strategy to exceed some specified minimum dollar amount. This would ensure that our optimal strategy would generate a minimum dollar amount of daily income in an unchanged market environment. To calculate the value of the Greeks for a given strategy, we would compute the sum of: the number of contracts times the per contract Greek value across every option position in the strategy.

We should always determine the amount of capital we are willing to commit to a given strategy using position-sizing calculations that incorporate our personal level of risk tolerance and our total available capital. We would know the amount of capital that we would like to allocate to a hybrid income strategy, but the optimizer would not. As a result, we would need to include a constraint that limits the amount of required capital to a specific range of acceptable values. Without this constraint, the optimizer would continue to increase its position sizes if it finds a favorable solution. If you do not have a portfolio margin account, the amount of required capital would be determined by applying the FINRA margin requirements to the strategy solution.

If you use a portfolio margin account, then the required capital for the hybrid strategy would be a function of the stress-testing algorithm used by your brokerage firm. For option strategies on broad-market equity indices, most brokerage firms would stress test your position assuming an instantaneous change in the price of the underlying equity index of plus and minus 8% to 10%. The amount of capital required would be the maximum loss incurred by your portfolio in your broker's worst case scenario. Consult your brokerage firm for its specific portfolio margin methodology.

In addition to limiting the total amount of required capital for the strategy, we also might want to limit the maximum number of contracts for each individual position for liquidity purposes. This would require one constraint for each adjustable purchase and sales variable.

We explored the possibility of adding probability-weighted changes in strategy values or probability-weighted Greek Effects to the objective function, but we could also further refine the optimization by adding scenario value constraints or risk/return ratio constraints as well. Including probability-weighted scenario values in the objective function would not prevent an individual scenario from delivering unacceptable results.

To eliminate this possibility, we could add constraints to force each scenario value to exceed a specified value. For example, we could require the maximum loss in any scenario to be no worse than 10% of the required capital. We could implement similar constraints for the minimum acceptable risk/return ratio at each price level. One constraint would be required for each scenario or price level.

Many other types of constraints and objective function elements could be used to further customize the process and to give you even more control over strategy optimization. There is a great deal of science and mathematics supporting solution algorithms, but setting up an optimization problem is an art. The problem should be designed to meet your specific needs.

Optimization Software Platform

There are a wide range of optimization tools available, but we would be attempting to solve a very specific type of problem and not all tools would be applicable. Depending on the number of candidates that you would like to include in your analysis, the resulting problem could be quite large, especially if you would like to include weekly and monthly option candidates for a wide range of strike prices.

In addition, this optimization problem would include formulas that are non-linear. This would make it much more difficult for the optimization algorithm to find the optimal solution. The software would need to distinguish between local and global optimums and would need to take explicit steps to find the optimal global solution.

Finally, the adjustable variables would be limited to integers, not real numbers. This would make it even more challenging for the algorithm and would further limit the number of potential software alternatives.

I am using the same optimization software that I used when I was a fixed-income institutional portfolio manager. The name of the optimization software is "What's Best" and it is available through Lindo Systems in Chicago. The What's Best software is an Excel add-in, which greatly enhances its versatility. The software is offered at different price levels, which correspond to the maximum number of permissible constraints and variables. What's Best can solve integer problems, but add-on modules would be required to find non-linear and non-linear global solutions.

Developing the capability to optimize option income strategies would require a substantial commitment of time and resources, but the potential benefits would be extraordinary, especially when integrated with the risk/return ratios introduced in this book. I have only been using the formal optimization process for a short time, but have already uncovered very unique strategies that I never would have discovered without these tools. Using these new techniques has also greatly enhanced my knowledge of option income strategies.

The options market is becoming increasingly efficient and very few individual traders have access to these types of tools. Institutional investment managers have virtually unlimited resources, but the size of their portfolios prevents them from employing most types of option income strategies. They are simply too big for the market. As a result, using these types of sophisticated tools can generate significant excess returns for individual traders who are willing to dedicate the resources to cultivate a market edge.

Conclusion

This is the first time the pivotal concepts of risk and return have been integrated successfully into a consistent approach for managing option income strategies. The risk/return ratios introduced in this book will allow you to evaluate, compare, adjust, and even optimize any option income strategy, on any underlying security, in any market environment.

This revolutionary new risk/return framework will help you reduce the risk and increase the prospective returns of all of your option income strategies. It will expose the strengths and weaknesses of conventional strategies and assist you in creating strategies with the lowest levels of risk per unit of return. When used in conjunction with optimization tools, this approach will even uncover exciting new hybrid strategies, customized to meet your specific strategy needs.

Thank you for investing your time and effort to review the many new and challenging concepts presented in the last 13 chapters. I hope you found the risk/return ratios and the insights in this book to be helpful and I hope they greatly enhance your ability to construct and manage your option income strategies. Good luck in your trading.

ABOUT THE AUTHOR

Brian Johnson designed, programmed, and implemented the first return sensitivity based parametric framework actively used to control risk in fixed income portfolios. He further extended the capabilities of this approach by designing and programming an integrated series of option valuation, prepayment, and optimization models.

Based on this technology, Mr. Johnson founded Lincoln Capital Management's fixed income index business, where he ultimately managed over $13 billion in assets for some of the largest and most sophisticated institutional clients in the U.S. and around the globe.

He later served as the President of a financial consulting and software development firm, designing artificial intelligence-based forecasting and risk management systems for institutional investment managers.

Mr. Johnson is now a full-time proprietary trader in options, futures, stocks, and ETFs primarily using algorithmic trading strategies. In addition to his professional investment experience, he also designed and taught courses in financial derivatives for both MBA and undergraduate business programs.

His second book, *Exploiting Earnings Volatility: An Innovative New Approach to Evaluating, Optimizing, and Trading Option Strategies to Profit from Earnings Announcements,* was published in 2015. He has also written articles for the *Financial Analysts Journal, Active Trader,* and *Seeking Alpha* and he regularly shares his trading insights and research ideas as the editor of www.TraderEdge.Net.

Mr. Johnson holds a B.S. degree in finance with high honors from the University of Illinois at Urbana-Champaign and an MBA degree with a specialization in Finance from the University of Chicago Booth School of Business.

Email: BJohnson@TraderEdge.Net

RESOURCES

I write a wide range of free, informative articles on www.TraderEdge.Net. The goal of Trader Edge is to provide information and ideas that will help you enhance your investment process and improve your trading results. The articles cover a wide range of topics: economic indicators, technical analysis, market commentary, options, futures, stocks, exchange traded funds (ETFs), strategy development, trade analysis, and risk management. You will find educational articles that appeal to the beginner, as well as advanced tools and strategies to support more experienced traders.

Trader Edge also offers a subscription to one of the proprietary strategies that I developed and trade in my own account. The Trader Edge Asset Allocation Rotational (AAR) Strategy is a conservative, long-only, asset allocation strategy that rotates monthly among five large asset classes: large-cap U.S. stocks, developed country stocks in Europe and Asia, emerging market stocks, U.S. Treasury Notes, and commodities. The strategy was inspired by the "Ivy League portfolio" and uses trend and technical filters to reduce downside risk. The AAR strategy has generated approximately 20% annual returns over the 20+ year combined back and forward test period. Please visit www.TraderEdge.Net to learn more about the AAR strategy.

Trading options without a comprehensive option analytical platform is not advisable and the OptionVue software is one of the most powerful tools available. Unlike most broker platforms, OptionVue evaluates both the horizontal and vertical volatility skews, resulting in much more realistic calculations and more accurate risk and valuation metrics. OptionVue also offers historical and real-time option prices.

Through our referral agreement, OptionVue is offering an exclusive 15% discount on the initial purchase of any annual subscription of any OptionVue product and on all DiscoverOptions educational products. However, the discount is not available to current OptionVue clients with an active OptionVue subscription. Please use the coupon code "traderedge" (*lower case with no spaces or quotation marks*) to receive your 15% discount when ordering applicable products from OptionVue online or over the phone.

I encourage you to visit the OptionVue referral page:

http://www.optionvue.com/traderedge.html and take advantage of the exclusive 15% Trader Edge referral discount. If you would prefer to evaluate the OptionVue software before placing an order, the above link will also allow you to enroll in a free 14-day trial of OptionVue's option analytical platform.

OptionSlam.com is one of the premier sites for tradable earnings information. I encourage you to visit the Optionslam.com referral page: https://www.optionslam.com/partner_info/traderedge and take advantage of the exclusive 15% Trader Edge referral discount. Note the underscore ("_") between "partner" and "info" in the above link.

Reliable prices are essential for developing and implementing systematic trading strategies. Commodity Systems Inc. (CSI) is one of the leading providers of market data and trading software for institutional and retail customers: https://csicheckout.com/cgi-bin/ua_order_form_nw.pl?referrer=TE.

I am a paying customer of OptionSlam.com, OptionVue, and CSI. My company, Trading Insights, LLC, has an affiliate referral relationship with OptionSlam.com, OptionVue, and CSI.

Purchasing this book entitles you to download and use the associated risk/return Excel spreadsheet for your own research. However, you may not transfer or share copies of the spreadsheet, passwords, or download links with others.

There are XLS (Office 2003-2007) and XLSM (Office 2010 or later) versions of the spreadsheet available for download; both contain macros. *If you experience any problems opening or running the XLSM file, download the XLS file instead.* The spreadsheets are included in encrypted zip files. Many cells in the spreadsheet are protected or validated to ensure the formulas function correctly. However, you may still use the worksheets interactively to analyze any of your option income strategies.

To download one or both of the zip files, go to **http://traderedge.net/rrr-spreadsheets-2/** and follow the download instructions. You will need a recent version of WinZip or a compatible utility to access the files.

You will need the following case-specific password to unencrypt the zip files: UnlockRRRZip647236

You will also need a separate case-specific password to open the Excel files: TraderEdge.NetRRR1

If for any reason the Trader Edge website were not accessible, please send me an email (BJohnson@TraderEdge.Net) with a copy of your electronic receipt for the purchase of this book and I will send you a copy of the zip file as an email attachment.

Made in the USA
San Bernardino, CA
27 May 2015